MATH GAMES
FOR THE COMMON CORE

Grade 3

Operations • Algebraic Thinking • Base Ten • Fractions

Warm Up

Explain

Differentiate

Support

Challenge

Understand

Gail Gerdemann with Kathleen Barta

Order Number 211081
ISBN 978-1-58324-660-3

C D E F G 21 20 19 18 17

395 Main Street
Rowley, MA 01969
www.didax.com

Table of Contents

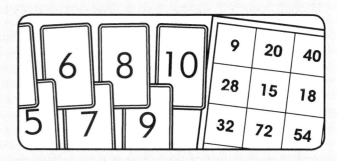

Teacher Notes

Introduction

Math Games for the Common Core targets these domains of the Grade 3 Common Core State Standards:

- Operations and Algebraic Thinking
- Number and Operations in Base Ten
- Number and Operations—Fractions

These games are designed to help students understand key concepts and strengthen skills. Developing number sense can take time. We all know that students are more engaged when they are having fun, and these games are designed for both substance and fun.

The *Math Games* program is also designed to be straightforward for teachers. Supplies include standard equipment like paper clips and colored markers, as well as copies of blackline masters. All materials for the year may be duplicated and organized in about one hour. Basic manipulatives such as tiles and fraction pieces are recommended but not required.

The animated presentation files involve students in reviewing the key concepts and mathematical vocabulary they will need to play the games. They also teach the students how to play each game. The visual approach of the presentation files and the differentiated games make this program ideal for all students, including English Language Learners and Tier II students.

Each game unit provides:

- Ideas for more support and for more challenge
- Discussion questions to help students:
    - Make connections between the game and mathematical concepts
    - Engage in CCSS Mathematical Practices
- Straightforward directions
- Blackline masters

These games may also be used for home-school activities. The presentation files will make family math events easy to organize. During family math gatherings, be sure to share the ideas for more support and more challenge with parents. They will appreciate understanding how to adapt the games to meet their children's special needs.

Teacher Notes

Materials

It will take approximately one hour with a high-speed copier and a paper cutter to prepare and organize a year's worth of materials for this program.

Step 1: Duplicate the blackline masters and place them in file folders.

Step 2: Duplicate cards on index-weight paper; cut the cards.

Step 3: Gather the recommended manipulatives.

Blackline masters (BLMs) begin on page 73. They are also on the CD.

Note on Number Cards: Regular playing cards may be substituted. Remove Kings, Jacks, and 10s. Use the Ace as 1 and the Queens as zero. ("Q" looks similar to "0.")

Bibliography

Carpenter, T., Fennema, E., Franke, M. L., Levi, L., & Empson, S. B. (1999). *Children's Mathematics: Cognitively Guided Instruction.* Portsmouth, NH: Heinemann.

Charles, R. I. (Ed.). (2010). *Developing Essential Understanding of Rational Numbers for Teaching Mathematics in Grades 3–5.* Reston, VA: National Council of Teachers of Mathematics.

Dougherty, B. J. (Ed.). (2011). *Developing Essential Understanding of Algebraic Thinking for Teaching Mathematics in Grades 3–5.* Reston, VA: National Council of Teachers of Mathematics.

Fosnot, C. T. (Ed.). (2010). *Models of Intervention in Mathematics: Reweaving the Tapestry.* Reston, VA: National Council of Teachers of Mathematics.

Fosnot, C. T., & Dolk, M. (2002). *Young Mathematicians at Work: Constructing Fractions, Decimals and Percents.* Portsmouth, NH: Heinemann.

Fosnot, C., & Dolk, M. (2001). *Young Mathematicians at Work: Constructing Multiplication and Division.* Portsmouth, NH: Heinemann.

Kilpatrick, J., Swafford, J., & Findell, B. (Eds.). (2001). *Adding It Up.* Washington, D.C.: National Academy Press.

Kitchen, R. S., & Silver, E. A. (Eds.). (2010). *Assessing English Language Learners in Mathematics, A Research Monograph of TODOS: Mathematics for All.* Washington, D.C.: National Education Association.

Rathmell, E. C. (Ed.). (2011). *Developing Essential Understanding of Multiplication and Division for Teaching Mathematics in Grades 3–5.* Reston, VA: National Council of Teachers of Mathematics.

Van De Walle, J., Karp, K., & Bay-Williams, J. (2010). *Elementary and Middle School Mathematics.* New York: Allyn & Bacon.

Teacher Notes

Standards Overview for *Math Games for the Common Core (Grade 3)*

Mathematical Content (Common Core State Standards for Grade 3)	Games											
	3-1	3-2	3-3	3-4	3-5	3-6	3-7	3-8	3-9	3-10	3-11	3-12
Operations and Algebraic Thinking												
Understand properties of multiplication and the relationship between multiplication and division. (3.OA.5–6)	✓					✓						
Multiply and divide within 100. (3.OA.7)		✓		✓	✓		✓		✓			
Solve problems involving the four operations and identify and explain patterns in arithmetic. (3.OA.8–9)		✓	✓									
Number and Operations in Base Ten												
Use place value understanding and properties of operations to perform multidigit arithmetic.							✓	✓	✓	✓		
Number and Operations – Fractions												
Develop an understanding of fractions as numbers. (3.NF.1–3)											✓	✓
CCSS Standards for Mathematical Practice												
1. Make sense of problems and persevere in solving them.	✓	✓	✓	✓	✓	✓	✓	✓	✓	✓	✓	✓
2. Reason abstractly and quantitatively.					✓	✓	✓	✓	✓	✓	✓	✓
3. Construct viable arguments and critique the reasoning of others.				✓			✓	✓	✓	✓		
4. Model with mathematics.												✓
5. Use appropriate tools strategically.												
6. Attend to precision.												
7. Look for and make use of structure.	✓	✓	✓	✓	✓			✓		✓		
8. Look for and express regularity in repeated reasoning.				✓				✓	✓	✓		

About the Authors

Gail Gerdemann is a retired teacher from the Corvallis School District in Oregon. She was also the Elementary Science Technology Engineering Math (STEM) Specialist for Oregon State University (1994–2012). Currently Gail is a consultant with several Oregon school districts.

Kathleen Barta is a retired teacher from North Clackamas School District in Oregon. She also was an instructor in Curriculum and Instruction for the University of Portland for many years. Currently she is Director of Teacher to Teacher Publications, Inc.

Special thanks to . . .

Linda Griffin, who was a major contributor to and reviewer of this project. She contributed many ideas, particularly for differentiation, and assisted the authors in making sure each unit was not only grounded in the Common Core State Standards but also in the research on which those standards were based. Linda is the Program Director for Early Childhood and Elementary Education at Lewis and Clark College, Portland, Oregon. Previously, she was the Mathematics Education Unit Director for the Northwest Regional Educational Laboratory.

Double Trouble

Learning Objectives

Develop fluency with the multiplication facts for 2s and 4s.

Content Standards

Apply properties of operations as strategies to multiply . . . (CCSSM: 3.OA.5)

Fluently multiply . . . within 100, using strategies such as the relationship between multiplication and division . . . or properties of operations. By the end of Grade 3, know from memory all products of two one-digit numbers. (CCSSM: 3.OA.7)

Identify arithmetic patterns (including patterns in the addition table or multiplication table), and explain them using properties of operations. (CCSSM: 3.OA.9)

Prerequisite Skills

Students should be fluent, or nearly fluent, with adding one- and two-digit numbers within 100.

Math Vocabulary

double

Materials

For each pair of students:	Warm-Ups	"Double Trouble" Game	"Double Trouble – Four in a Row" Game
• Deck of Number Cards 0–10 (page 107)	✓	✓	✓
• Multiplication Chart (page 108)	✓	✓	
• Spinners (page 74)		✓	✓
• Game Board (page 75)			✓
• Tiles or other markers	✓		

Warm-Up A-1: Using Area Models for Multiples of 2

Materials for each pair of students:

- Tiles (at least 30)
- 1-cm graph paper (optional)

Directions:

1. Build area models with tiles for the first five multiples of 2 on a projector or whiteboard. Identify rows, columns, and dimensions.

2. Have each pair of students make models of the first five multiples of 2 with tiles. List the total number of tiles or units in each area model (save this list to use again):

Rows (How many rows)	Columns (How many tiles in each row)	2 × __ (2 groups of __)
2	1	2 × 1 = 2
2	2	2 × 2 = 4
2	3	2 × 3 = 6
2	4	2 × 4 = 8
2	5	2 × 5 = 10

3. Ask students what they notice about the pattern. (They may note the pattern of even numbers; each multiple is 2 more than the previous one.)

4. Physically turn the area models 90 degrees and record the rows, columns, and equations to illustrate the commutative property of multiplication.

5. Students who are being introduced to multiplication, or students who need more support, need to spend time working with visual representations before completing the list of multiples of 2 through 2 × 10. Have them:

   - Fold two pieces of graph paper in half the long way (hotdog fold).

   - Sketch area models of 2 × 1 through 2 × 10 on graph paper on the left side of their papers, leaving some space between each sketch.

   - Label the dimensions. Write an equation to represent each area model (for example, 2 × 3 = 6).

   - On the right side of their papers, show each model turned 90 degrees. Label the dimensions and the total number of units for each model.

   - Circle each pair of equations with the same product. (For example, circle 2 × 5 = 10 and 5 × 2 = 10.)

   - Complete the list of the multiples of 2 through 2 × 10.

Warm-Up A-2: Skip–Count by 2s

Directions:

1. Whole class stands in a circle.
2. Players take turns skip counting by 2s, one number at a time. Whoever says "20" sits down.
3. Anyone who sits down is now a judge and needs to verify that the correct number has been called out.
4. The next player begins again with "2." Game continues until only one student is left.

(*Note:* In the Differentiation section, see the reference to songs for multiples.)

Warm-Up A-3: Product Crossing with Twos

Number of Players: 2

Materials:

• Deck of Number Cards 0–10 (page 107)

Object: Cross off each of the numbers on the list of products by multiplying correctly and quickly.

Directions:

1. Each player makes a list of the products of 2 (0, 2, 4, … , 20) and then turns the list facedown.
2. Place the first factor card, 2, on the table.
3. Players take turns:
   • Drawing a card from the deck (This is the other factor.)
   • Multiplying the number on the card by 2.
4. If players say the product correctly and quickly, they cross it off their list of products and then turn the list facedown again.
5. Players reshuffle the cards as needed. The first player to cross off all the numbers on his/her list of products wins.

Warm-Up B-1: Using Area Models for Multiples of 4

Materials:

For a projection device:
- Multiplication Chart (page 108)

For each pair of students:
- Tiles (at least 30)
- 1-cm graph paper (optional)

Directions:

1. Build area models with tiles for the first three multiples of 4 on a projector or whiteboard.

2. Have each pair of students use tiles to make an area model for each of the first five multiples of 4.

3. As a class, record the rows, columns, and total number of units for each multiple of 4 next to the information for the corresponding multiple of 2:

Rows	Columns	2 × __ (2 groups of __)	4 × __ (4 groups of __)	Columns	Rows
2	1	$2 \times 1 = 2$	$4 \times 1 = 4$	1	4
2	2	$2 \times 2 = 4$	$4 \times 2 = 8$	2	4
2	3	$2 \times 3 = 6$	$4 \times 3 = 12$	3	4
2	4	$2 \times 4 = 8$	$4 \times 4 = 16$	4	4
2	5	$2 \times 5 = 10$	$4 \times 5 = 20$	5	4

4. Ask students what they notice about the pattern. (If necessary, ask questions to help students discover that each area model for a multiple of 4 is twice as large as the matching model.)

5. Look at a multiplication chart. Highlight all the multiples of 2 and 4. Ask students if the pattern(s) they noticed work for all the multiples of 4.

6. Students who are being introduced to multiplication, or students who need more support, should spend time working with visual representations before completing the list of multiples of 4 through 4 × 10. Have them:

- Fold two pieces of graph paper in half the long way (hotdog fold).

- Sketch area models of 4 × 1 through 4 × 10 on graph paper on the left side of their papers, leaving some space between each area model.

- Label the dimensions. Write an equation to represent each area model (for example, 4 × 6 = 24).

- On the right side of their papers, show each model turned 90°. Label the dimensions and total number of units for each model.

- Circle each pair of equations with the same product. For example, circle 4 × 5 = 20 and 5 × 4 = 20.

Warm-Up B-2: Skip-Count by 4s

Directions:

1. Whole class stands in a circle.

2. Players take turns skip counting by 4s, one number at a time. Whoever says "40" sits down.

3. Anyone who sits down is now a judge and needs to verify that the correct number has been called out.

4. The next player begins again with "4." Game continues until only one student is left.

 # Warm-Up B-3: Double 2s

Number of Players: Pairs of students

Materials:

• Deck of Number Cards 0–10 (page 107)

Object: Practice multiplying by 2s and 4s.

Directions:

1. Player 1 draws a card and multiplies that number by 2.

2. Player 2 multiplies the same number by 4, doubling the "2 ×" product. Example: Player 1 draws "5" and says, "2 × 5 = 10." Player 2 says, "4 × 5 = 20."

3. Partners check each other's answers for accuracy.

4. Students alternate being Player 1.

Warm-Up B-4: Product Crossing with 4s

Number of Players: 2

Materials:

- Deck of Number Cards 0–10 (page 107)

Object: Cross off each of the numbers on the list of products by multiplying correctly and quickly.

Directions:

1. Each player makes a list of the products of 4 (0, 4, 8, . . . , 40) and then turns the list facedown.

2. Place the first factor card, 4, on the table.

3. Students take turns:
   - Drawing a card from the deck. This is the other factor.
   - Multiplying the number on the card by 4.

4. If players say the product correctly and quickly, they cross it off their list of products and then turn the list facedown again.

5. Players reshuffle the cards as needed. The first player to cross off all the numbers on his/her list of products wins.

Explaining the Game: Double Trouble

Number of Players: 2

Materials:

For each pair of students:

- Two Spinners (page 74)
- Deck of Number Cards 0–10 (page 107)
- Multiplication Chart (facedown, except when used to check products) (page 108)
- Game Rules, if needed, after presentation (page 1119)

Object: Players multiply their "spinner number" by the number on their card. Larger (or smaller) product wins.

How to Play:

1. Each player:
   - Spins for his/her "spinner number."
   - Draws a number card from the deck.
   - Multiplies the "spinner number" by the number on his/her card.
   - Says the equation (for example, "2 times 7 equals 14").

2. The player with the larger product wins both cards.

3. Repeat until the deck is used up. The player with the most cards wins.

4. Shuffle the cards and play again. Smaller product wins.

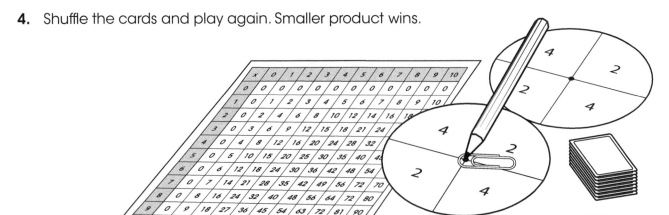

Variations

- Flip a coin to determine the winner (heads: larger product; tails: smaller product).
- Use only one spinner. The first player to say the product correctly wins.

Explaining the Game: Double Trouble – Four in a Row

Number of Players: Pairs of students

Materials:

For each pair of students:
- "Double Trouble – Four in a Row" Game Board (page 75)
- 4 sets of the Number Cards 2 and 4
- Tiles or other markers
- Game Rules, if needed, after presentation (page 120)

Object: Multiply to capture four adjacent numbers in a row (horizontal, vertical, or diagonal).

Directions:

1. Players take turns drawing a card.

2. The player whose turn it is:
   - Multiplies the number on the card by one of the factors at the top of the page.
   - Says the multiplication fact and places a tile on the product.

3. If that product has already been captured, it is the other player's turn.

4. The first player to capture four adjacent numbers in a row wins.

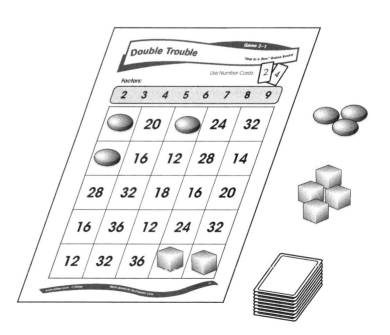

Differentiation

Warm-Up Exercises A-1 and B-1

More Support

- Build all the models with tiles. Some students may need to begin by counting to figure out how many tiles are in each array. They may need to do this many times before they understand and learn the multiples.

- Songs help some students learn the multiples. Songs for the multiples of 2 through 6 are available at **www.teachertoteacher.com/songs.html**. Video clips are included.

"Double Trouble" Game

More Support

- At first, limit the number cards to 0–5 when playing "Double Trouble." Then gradually add the other number cards to the deck.

- Allow students to use their grid paper arrays as references, if needed.

*More Challenge
(Above grade level)*

- Draw a card to determine the starting number. Take turns doubling, mentally if possible, until one player, the winner, crosses the 100 mark.

"Double Trouble – Four in a Row" Game

More Support

- Play cooperatively. Goal can be to get five in a row or to capture every square (blackout).

More Challenge

- Play competitively. The winner gets 20 points for being the first to get four in a row, but subtracts 1 point for each tile he/she played that is not in the winning row. The other player gets one point for each tile played.

- Create a game board for the factors 2–10 and the cards 2 and 4. Play the game.

Deepening the Understanding

Ask the class:	Mathematical Practices (CCSSM)	
(Show a multiplication chart.)	MP2	Reason abstractly and quantitatively.
What patterns or relationships could help someone when they need to multiply by:	MP7	Look for and make use of structure.
0?		
1?		
2?		
4?		
(Show a multiplication chart with the 2s and 4s shaded in.)	MP2	Reason abstractly and quantitatively.
Look for patterns/relationships among the products of 2 and 4:	MP7	Look for and make use of structure.
• Which products do you see more than once? Why do they show up more than once?		
• What are some strategies or relationships that help you remember the products of 2 and 4? What are some other strategies?		

Think About 10

Learning Objectives

Use the decade strategy to multiply numbers by 10, 5, and 9 and gain fluency. Review multiplication facts for the 4s.

Content Standards

Fluently multiply . . . within 100, using strategies such as the relationship between multiplication and division . . . or properties of operations. By the end of Grade 3, know from memory all products of two one-digit numbers. (CCSSM: 3.OA.7)

Identify arithmetic patterns (including patterns in the addition table or multiplication table), and explain them using properties of operations. (CCSSM: 3.OA.9)

Prerequisite Skills

Students should be fluent, or nearly fluent, with adding one- and two-digit numbers within 100. They should be developing fluency with multiplication facts for 2s and 4s.

Math Vocabulary

half

Materials

For each pair of students:	Warm-Ups	"Think About 10" Game	"Think About 10 – Four in a Row" Game
• Deck of Number Cards 0–10 (page 107)	✓	✓	✓
• Area Models of 10 × 1–10 × 9 (pages 76–77)	✓		
• Multiplication Chart (page 108)		✓	
• Spinners (page 78)		✓	
• Game Boards (pages 79–80)			✓
• Markers	✓		
• Tiles			✓

Warm-Up A-1: Using Area Models for Multiples of 10

Materials:

For a projection device:

- Area Models for 10 × 1 through 10 × 5 (page 76)

For each student:

- Area Models for 10 × 1 through 10 × 5 (page 76)

Directions:

1. Show area models for 10 × 1 through 10 × 5.

2. Identify rows, columns, and dimensions.

3. Hand out the "Area Models" page to each pair of students.

4. Tell students to complete the equations, showing the total number of units in each area model.

5. As a class, record the rows, columns, and total number of units in each area model. Record this list to keep for future work.

Rows (How many rows)	Columns (How many tiles in each row)	10 × __ (10 groups of __)
10	1	10 × 1 = 10
10	2	10 × 2 = 20
10	3	10 × 3 = 30
10	4	10 × 4 = 40
10	5	10 × 5 = 50

6. Ask students what they notice about the pattern. (They may note that each multiple ends in a zero and that each multiple is 10 more than the previous one.)

7. Complete the list of the multiples of 10 through 10 × 10.

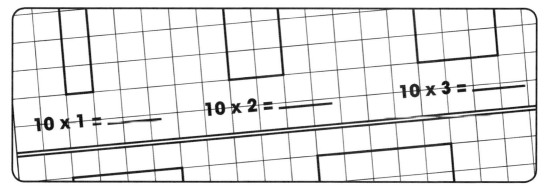

10 × 1 = _____   10 × 2 = _____   10 × 3 = _____

Warm-Up B-1: Using Area Models for Multiples of 5

Materials:

For a projection device:
- Area Models for 10 × 1 through 10 × 5 (page 76)

For each pair of students:
- Area Models for 10 × 1 through 10 × 5 (page 76, from Exercise A-1)
- Area Models of 10 × 6 through 10 × 9 (optional, page 77: see differentiation page)
- Colored markers

Directions:

1. Show the area models for 10 × 1 through 10 × 5 on a projector.

2. Ask a student to:
   - Color an area model for 5 × 1 on the lower part of the model for 10 × 1, then color 5 × 2 on the lower part of the model for 10 × 2, and so on.
   - Write the equation on the area model for each multiple of 5.

3. Tell students to:
   - Color area models for the first five multiples of 5 on the matching areas of the "'Think About 10' Area Models for 10 × 1 through 10 × 5" page.
   - Write the equation for each "5 ×" area model.

4. As a class, record the rows, columns, and total number of units for each multiple of 5 next to the information for the corresponding multiple of 10:

Rows	Columns	10 × __ (10 groups of __)	5 × __ (5 groups of __)	Columns	Rows
10	1	10 × 1 = 10	5 × 1 = 5	1	5
10	2	10 × 2 = 20	5 × 2 = 10	2	5
10	3	10 × 3 = 30	5 × 3 = 15	3	5
10	4	10 × 4 = 40	5 × 4 = 20	4	5
10	5	10 × 5 = 50	5 × 5 = 25	5	5

5. Ask students what they notice about the pattern. If necessary, ask questions to help students discover that each area model for a multiple of 5 is half as large as the matching area model for the multiple of 10—or the product of 5 × *a* is half of the product of 10 × *a*.

6. Look at a multiplication chart. Highlight all the multiples of 5 and all the multiples of 10. Ask students if the pattern they noticed works for all the multiples of 10.

Warm-Up B-2: Half of 10s

Materials:

- Deck of Number Cards 0–10 (page 107)

Directions:

1. Students work with a partner to practice multiplying by 10s and 5s.
2. Player 1 draws a number card and multiplies it by 10.
3. Player 2 multiplies the same digit by 5 (half of the "10 ×" product).

   For example:

   Player 1 draws "6" and says, "10 × 6 = 60."

   Player 2 says, "6 × 5 = 30."
4. Partners check each other's work for accuracy.
5. Students alternate being Player 1.

Warm-Up B-3: Product Crossing with Fives

Number of Players: 2

Materials:

- Deck of Number Cards 0–10 (page 107)

Object: Cross off each of the numbers on the list of products by multiplying correctly and quickly.

Directions:

1. Each player makes a list of the products of 5 (0, 5, 10, . . . , 50) and then turns the list facedown.
2. Place the first factor card, 5, on the table.
3. Students take turns:
   - Drawing a card from the deck. This is the other factor.
   - Multiplying the number on the card by 5.
4. If players say the product correctly and quickly, they cross it off their list of products and then turn the list facedown again.
5. Players reshuffle the cards as needed. The first player to cross off all the numbers on his/her list of products wins.

Warm-Up C–1: Multiplying by 9

Materials:

For a projection device:
- Area Models for 10 x 1 through 10 x 5 (page 76)

For each pair of students:
- Area Models for 10 x 1 through 10 x 5 (page 76)
- Colored markers

Directions:

1. Show the Area Models for 10 x 1 through 10 x 5 on a projector.

2. Ask a student to:
   - Color an area model for 9 x 1 on the lower part of the model for 10 x 1, color an area model for 9 x 2 on the lower part of the model for 10 x 2, and so on.
   - Write the equation on the area model for each multiple of 9.

3. Tell students to:
   - Color area models for the first five multiples of 9 in the matching areas on the "Area Models for the First Five Multiples of 10" page.
   - Write the equation for each "9 x" area model.

4. As a class, record the rows, columns, and total number of units for each multiple of 9 next to the information for the corresponding multiple of 10:

Rows	Columns	10 x ___ (10 groups of ___)	9 x ___ (9 groups of ___)	Columns	Rows
10	1	10 x 1 = 10	9 x 1 = 9	1	9
10	2	10 x 2 = 20	9 x 2 = 18	2	9
10	3	10 x 3 = 30	9 x 3 = 27	3	9
10	4	10 x 4 = 40	9 x 4 = 36	4	9
10	5	10 x 5 = 50	9 x 5 = 45	5	9

5. Ask students what they notice about the pattern. If necessary, ask questions to help students discover that each area model for a multiple of 9 has one less row than the matching area model for a multiple of 10, and that the product of 9 x a is equal to 10 x a − a.

6. Look at a multiplication chart. Highlight all the multiples of 9 and multiples of 10. Ask students if the pattern they noticed works for all the multiples of 9.

Warm-Up C-2: 10s and 9s

Number of Players: 2

Object: Practice multiplying by 10s and 9s.

Materials:

- Deck of Number Cards 0–10 (page 107)

Directions:

1. Player 1 draws a card and multiplies that number by 10.
2. Player 2 multiplies the same number by 9. (It is the "10 ×" product minus the number card number.)

   For example:

   Player 1 draws 6 and says, "10 × 6 = 60."

   Player 2 says, "60 – 6 = 54, so 9 × 6 = 54."

3. Players check each other's answers for accuracy.
4. Students alternate being Player 1.

Warm-Up C-3: Product Crossing with Nines

Number of Players: 2

Materials:

- Deck of Number Cards 0–10 (page 107)

Object: Cross off each of the numbers on the list of products by multiplying correctly and quickly.

Directions:

1. Each player makes a list of the products of 9 (0, 9, 18, . . . , 90) and then turns the list facedown.
2. Place the first factor card, 9, on the table.
3. Students take turns:
   - Drawing a card from the deck. This is the other factor.
   - Multiplying the number on the card by 9.
4. If players say the product correctly and quickly, they cross it off their list of products and then turn the list facedown again.
5. Players reshuffle the cards as needed. The first player to cross off all the numbers on his/her list of products wins.

◯ Explaining the Game: Think About 10

Number of Players: 2

Materials:

For each pair of students:

- Two Spinners (page 78)
- Deck of Number Cards 0–10 (page 107)
- Multiplication Chart (facedown, except when used to check products) (page 108)
- Game Rules, if needed, after presentation (page 121)

Object: Players multiply their "spinner number" by the number on their card. Larger (or smaller) product wins.

How to Play:

1. Each player:
   - Spins for his/her "spinner number."
   - Draws a number card from the deck.
   - Multiplies the "spinner number" by the number on his/her card.
   - Says the equation (for example, 9 times 3 equals 27").

2. The player with the larger product wins both cards.

3. Repeat until the deck is used up. The player with the most cards wins.

4. Shuffle the cards and play again. Smaller product wins.

Explaining the Game: Think About 10 – Four in a Row

Number of Players: 2

Materials:

For each pair of students:
- 4 sets of the Number Cards 4, 5, 9, and 10
- "Think About 10 – Four in a Row" Game Board A (page 79)
- "Think About 10 – Four in a Row" Game Board B (optional, page 80)
- Game Rules, if needed, after presentation (page 122)
- Tiles or other markers

Object: Multiply to capture four adjacent numbers in a row (horizontal, vertical, or diagonal).

How to Play:

1. Players take turns drawing a card.

2. The player whose turn it is:
   - Multiplies the number on the card by one of the factors at the top of the page.
   - Says the multiplication fact and places a tile on the product.

3. If that product has already been captured, it is the other player's turn.

4. The first player to capture four adjacent numbers in a row wins.

   (*Note:* Game Board B is provided for more support. Only the factors 1–6 are used with cards 2, 5, 9, and 10.)

Differentiation

Warm-Up Activities A-1, B-1, and C-1

More Support

- Particularly for the multiples of 9 (Warm-Up C-1), some students may need to use the area models throughout the unit to better understand the relationship between the multiples of 10 and 9. (See "Area Models of 10 × 6 through 10 × 9," page 77.) Have students use those area models as a base from which to color additional multiples of 9 and/or 5. Time spent with area models that can be used for reference can help prevent confusion.

- Songs help some students learn the multiples. Songs for the multiples of 2 through 6 are available at **www.teachertoteacher.com/songs.html.** Video clips are included.

"Think About 10" Game

More Support

- Use the Area Models pages (76–77) from the Warm-Ups as a reference.

- Initially limit the spinner to 5 and 10. Later, include the 9, or

- Initially limit the Number Cards to 0–5 when playing this game. Then gradually add the other Number Cards to the deck.

"Think About 10 – Four in a Row" Game

More Support

- Game Board B is provided as an initial board. Only the factors 1–6 are used with cards 2, 5, 9, and 10.

- Play cooperatively. The goal can be to get five in a row or to capture every square ("blackout").

More Challenge

- Students create a game board for the factors 2–10 and the cards 4, 5, and 9, and then play the game.

Deepening the Understanding

Ask the class:	**Mathematical Practices (CCSSM)**
Highlight the multiples of 5, 10, and 9, each in a different color, on a multiplication chart.	MP2 Reason abstractly and quantitatively.
	MP7 Look for and make use of structure.

Highlight the multiples of 5, 10, and 9, each in a different color, on a multiplication chart.

~ What patterns do you see in the ones and tens places in the list of multiples of 9?

~ How many of the multiples of 5 are also multiples of 10? How many of the multiples of 5 are also multiples of 9?

~ Explain the difference between these comparisons.

~ Which numbers are highlighted in all three colors? Explain why this is so.

~ Look at each multiple of 9 (9×1 to 9×10). What patterns do you notice?

Triple Trouble

Learning Objectives

Develop fluency with the multiplication facts for 3s and 6s. Review multiplication facts for the 4s and 9s.

Content Standards

Apply properties of operations as strategies to multiply . . . (CCSSM: 3.OA.5)

Fluently multiply . . . within 100, using strategies such as the relationship between multiplication and division . . . or properties of operations. By the end of Grade 3, know from memory all products of two one-digit numbers. (CCSSM: 3.OA.7)

Identify arithmetic patterns (including patterns in the addition table or multiplication table), and explain them using properties of operations. (CCSSM: 3.OA.9)

Prerequisite Skills

Students should be developing fluency with multiplication facts for the 2s, 4s, 5s, 9s, and 10s. They should be fluent, or nearly fluent, with adding one- and two-digit numbers within 100.

Math Vocabulary

even
odd

Materials

For each pair of students:	Warm-Ups	"Triple Trouble" Game	"Triple Trouble: Four in a Row" Game
• Deck of Number Cards 0–10 (page 107)	✓	✓	✓
• Multiplication Chart (page 108)	✓	✓	
• Spinners (pages 81–82)		✓	
• Game Board A (page 83)			✓
• Game Boards B & C (optional) (pages 84–85)			✓
• Tiles	✓		✓

x	0	1	2	3	4	5	6	7	8
0	0	0	0	0	0	0	0	0	0
1	0	1	2	3	4	5	6	7	8
	0	2	4	6	8	10	12	14	16

Warm-Up A-1: Using Area Models for Multiples of 3

Materials:

For each student:

- Tiles (45)
- 1-cm graph paper (optional)

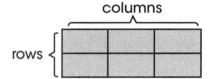

Directions:

1. Build area models with tiles for the first five multiples of 3 on a projector. Identify the rows, columns, and dimensions.

2. Have each pair of students make models of the first five multiples of 3 with tiles. List the total number of tiles or units in each area model:

Rows (How many rows)	Columns (How many tiles in each row)	3 × __ (3 groups of __)
3	1	3 × 1 = 3
3	2	3 × 2 = 6
3	3	3 × 3 = 9
3	4	3 × 4 = 12
3	5	3 × 5 = 15

3. Fold two pieces of graph paper in half the long way (hotdog fold).

4. Sketch area models of 3 × 1 through 3 × 10 on graph paper on the left side of their papers, leaving some space between each sketch.

5. Label the dimensions. Write an equation to represent each area model (for example, 3 × 4 = 12).

6. On the right side of their papers, show each model turned 90 degrees. Label the dimensions and the total number of units for each model.

7. Circle each pair of equations with the same product (for example, circle 3 × 5 = 15 and 5 × 3 = 15).

8. Complete the list of the multiples of 3 through 3 × 10.

Warm-Up A-2: Skip-Count by 3s

Directions:

1. Whole class stands in a circle.

2. Players take turns skip counting by 3s, one number at a time. Whoever says "30" sits down.

3. Anyone who sits down is now a judge and needs to verify that the correct number has been called out.

4. The next player begins again with "2." Game continues until only one student is left.

    (*Note:* In the Differentiation section, see the reference to songs for multiples.)

 # Warm-Up A-3: Product Crossing with 3s

Number of Players: 2

Materials: Deck of Number Cards 0–10 (page 107)

Object: Cross off each of the numbers on the list of products by multiplying correctly and quickly.

Directions:

1. Each player makes a list of the products of 3 (0, 3, 6, . . . , 30) and then turns the list facedown.

2. Place the first factor card, 3, on the table.

3. Players take turns:

    • Drawing a card from the deck. (This is the other factor.)

    • Multiplying the number on the card by 3.

4. If players say the product correctly and quickly, they cross it off their list of products and then turn the list facedown again.

5. Players reshuffle the cards as needed. The first player to cross off all the numbers on his/her list of products wins.

Warm-Up B-1: Using Area Models for Multiples of 6

Materials:

For a projection device:

     • Multiplication Chart (page 108)

For each pair of students:

     • Tiles (60)

     • Paper and pencils

Directions:

1. Build area models with tiles for the first three multiples of 6 on a projector.

2. Have each pair of students use tiles to make an area model for each of the first four multiples of 6.

3. As a class, record the rows, columns, and total number of units for each multiple of 6 next to the information for the corresponding multiple of 3:

Rows	Columns	3 × __ (3 groups of __)	6 × __ (6 groups of __)	Columns	Rows
3	1	3 × 1 = 3	6 × 1 = 6	1	6
3	2	3 × 2 = 6	6 × 2 = 12	2	6
3	3	3 × 3 = 9	6 × 3 = 18	3	6
3	4	3 × 4 = 12	6 × 4 = 24	4	6
3	5	3 × 5 = 15	6 × 5 = 30	5	6

4. Ask students what they notice about the pattern. (If necessary, ask questions to help students discover that each area model for a multiple of 6 is twice as large as the matching model for the multiple of 3. If needed, illustrate by placing contrasting tiles representing the multiples-of-3 models on top of the multiples-of-6 models.)

5. Look at a multiplication chart. Highlight all the multiples of 3 and 6. Ask students if the pattern(s) they noticed work for all the multiples of 6.

6. Without looking at a multiplication chart, complete the list of multiples of 6 through 6 × 10.

    (*Note:* See suggestions in the Differentiation section for students who need more support.

Warm-Up B-2: Double 3s

Number of Players: 2

Materials:
- Deck of Number Cards 0–10 (page 107)

Object: Practice multiplying by 3s and 6s.

Directions:
1. Player 1 draws a card and multiplies that number by 3.
2. Player 2 multiplies the same number by 6, doubling the "3 ×" product. For example, Player 1 draws "5" and says, "3 × 5 = 15." Player 2 says, "6 × 5 = 30."
3. Partners check each other's answers for accuracy.
4. Students alternate being Player 1.

Warm-Up B-3: Factor Crossing with 6s

Number of Players: 2

Materials:
- Deck of Number Cards 0–10 (page 107)

Object: Cross off each of the numbers on the list of products by multiplying correctly and quickly.

Directions:
1. Each player makes a list of the products of 6 (0, 6, 12, . . . , 60) and then turns the list facedown.
2. Place the first factor card, 6, on the table.
3. Students take turns:
   - Drawing a card from the deck. This is the other factor.
   - Multiplying the number on the card by 6.
4. If players say the product correctly and quickly, they cross it off their list of products and then turn the list facedown again.
5. Players reshuffle the cards as needed. The first player to cross off all the numbers on his/her list of products wins.

Explaining the Game: Triple Trouble

Number of Players: Pairs of students

Materials:

For each pair of students:
- 2 "Triple Trouble" Spinners (page 81)
- Deck of Number Cards 0–10 (page 107)
- Multiplication Chart (facedown, except when used to check products) (page 108)
- Game Rules, if needed, after presentation (page 123)

Object: Players multiply their "spinner number" by the number on their card. Larger (or smaller) product wins.

How to Play:

1. Each player:
   - Spins for his/her "spinner number."
   - Draws a number card from the deck.
   - Multiplies the "spinner number" by the number on his/her card.
   - Says the equation (for example, "6 times 7 equals 42").

2. The player with the larger product wins both cards.

3. Repeat until the deck is used up. The player with the most cards wins.

4. Shuffle the cards and play again. Smaller product wins.

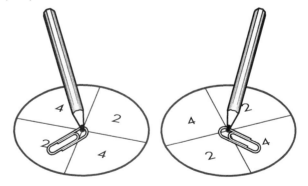

Variations

- Flip a coin to determine the winner (heads: larger product; tails: smaller product).
- Use the Alternate Spinner (multiples of 3, 4, 9, and 6) (page 82).

Explaining the Game: Triple Trouble – Four in a Row

Number of Players: 2

Materials:

For each pair of students:
- "Triple Trouble – Four in a Row" Game Board A (page 83)
- Deck of Number Cards 2–9 (page 107)
- Tiles or other markers
- Game Boards B and C (optional, pages 84–85)
- Game Rules, if needed, after presentation (page 124)

Object: Multiply to capture four adjacent numbers in a row (horizontal, vertical, or diagonal).

How to Play:

1. Players take turns drawing a card.

2. The player whose turn it is:
   - Multiplies the number on the card by one of the factors at the top of the game board.
   - Says the multiplication fact and places a tile on the product.

3. If that product has already been captured, it is the other player's turn.

4. The first player to capture four adjacent numbers in a row wins.

Variations
- Game Board B – multiples of 3, 4, 5, and 6 with factors 2–6 (easier)
- Game Board C – multiples of 3, 4, 6, and 9 with factors 2–9

Differentiation

Warm-Up Activities A-1 and B-1

More Support

- Have students sketch, label the dimensions, and write expressions (e.g., 3×7) to represent the factors for all the area models on 1-cm graph paper. Have students write the products on the back.

- Songs help some students learn the multiples. Songs for the multiples of 2 through 6 are available at www.teachertoteacher.com/songs.html. Video clips are included.

"Triple Trouble" Game

More Support

- Initially limit the number cards to 0–5 when playing this game. Then gradually add the other number cards to the deck.

- Allow students to use their graph paper arrays as references if needed.

"Triple Trouble – Four in a Row" Game

More Support

- Play cooperatively. Goal could be to get five in a row or to capture every square ("blackout").

- Use Game Board B, initially, to practice with the factors 2–6.

More Challenge

- Create a game board for the factors 2–10 and the cards 3, 4, 6, and 9. Play the game.

Deepening the Understanding

Ask the class:	Mathematical Practices (CCSSM)
(Show a multiplication chart, with the multiples of 3 and 6 shaded.) Look for additional patterns/relationships among the multiples of 3 and 6: ~ Do the digits in the ones place "cycle" as the factors increase? ~ Besides doubling threes, what other strategies or relationships can help you remember the multiples of 6? ~ How could knowing a twos fact help you find the related threes fact? How could 2×8 help you find 3×8? ~ How could knowing a twos facts help you find a sixes fact? How could 2×7 help you find 6×7?	MP2 Reason abstractly and quantitatively. MP7 Look for and make use of structure.
What strategy do you use to multiply by 6? Why does it work?	MP2 Reason abstractly and quantitatively. MP7 Look for and make use of structure.

Using Facts You Know

Learning Objectives

Develop fluency with the multiplication facts for 8s and 7s using a variety of methods, including using the facts you know to figure out other facts.

Content Standards

Apply properties of operations as strategies to multiply . . . (CCSSM: 3.OA.5)

Fluently multiply . . . within 100, using strategies such as the relationship between multiplication and division. . . or properties of operations. By the end of Grade 3, know from memory all products of two one-digit numbers. (CCSSM: 3.OA.7)

(*Note:* This unit is also correlated to CCSSM: 3.MD.7a–d.)

Prerequisite Skills

Students should be developing fluency with multiplication facts for 2s, 4s, 5s, 9s, and 10s. They should be at least nearly fluent with adding one- and two-digit numbers within 100.

Math Vocabulary

square numbers

Materials

For each pair of students:	Warm-Up	"Using the Facts . . ." Game	"Using the Facts – Four in a Row" Game
• Deck of Number Cards 0–10 (page 107)	✓	✓	✓
• "Chunk It" Recording Sheet – 2 copies (pages 86–87)	✓		
• Spinner (page 88)		✓	
• Multiplication Chart (page 108)		✓	
• Game Boards (pages 89–90)			✓
• Tiles or other markers			✓

Warm-Up A: Double Fours

Number of Players: 2

Materials: Deck of Number Cards 0–10 (page 107)

Object: Practice multiplying by 4s and 8s.

Directions:

1. Player 1 draws a card and multiplies that number by 4.

2. Player 2 multiplies the same number by 8 (doubling the "4 ×" product). For example:
   Player 1 draws "5" and says, "4 × 5 = 20."
   Player 2 says, "8 × 5 = 40."

3. Partners check each other's answers for accuracy.

4. Students alternate being Player 1.

Warm-Up B: Product Crossing with Eights

Number of Players: 2

Materials: Deck of Number Cards 0–10 (page 107)

Object: Cross off each of the numbers on the list of products by multiplying correctly and quickly.

Directions:

1. Each player makes a list of the products of 8 (0, 8, 16, . . . , 80) and then turns the list facedown.

2. Place the first factor card, 8, on the table.

3. Players take turns:
   • Drawing a card from the deck (This is the other factor.)
   • Multiplying the number on the card by 8.

4. If players say the product correctly and quickly, they cross it off their list of products and then turn the list facedown again.

5. Players reshuffle the cards as needed. The first player to cross off all the numbers on his/her list of products wins.

Warm-Up C: Chunk It

Number of Players: Pairs of students

Materials:

For each student:

- "Chunk It" Recording Sheet, pages 1 and 2 (pages 86–87)

Directions:

1. Working separately, each student:
   - Labels the dimensions of each area model on page 1 of the recording sheet.
   - Draws a line to make two chunks and finds the product of each chunk.
   - Adds the two products together to find the total product (area).
2. Working with partners or table groups, students compare their work.
3. Repeat using page 2 of the recording sheet.

4. Ask students with different types of solutions to share their work and their thinking.

Note: What to do about 7s?

We suggest two methods for figuring out the multiples of 7:

- Use the commutative property of multiplication. When given 7 × 4 =, use a known fact. Think, "4 × 7 = 28." Memorize "7 × 7 = 49."
- Use the "Chunk It" method.

 Warm-Up D: Product Crossing with Sevens

Number of Players: 2

Materials:

- Deck of Number Cards 0–10 (page 107)

Object: Cross off each of the numbers on the list of products by multiplying correctly and quickly.

Directions:

1. Each player makes a list of the products of 7 (0, 7, 14, . . . , 70) and then turns the list facedown.
2. Place the first factor card, 7, on the table.
3. Players take turns:
   - Drawing a card from the deck (This is the other factor.)
   - Multiplying the number on the card by 7.

4. If players say the product correctly and quickly, they cross it off their list of products and then turn the list facedown again.
5. Players reshuffle the cards as needed. The first player to cross off all the numbers on his/her list of products wins.

Explaining the Game: Using Facts You Know

Number of Players: 2

Materials:

For each pair of students:

- 2 "Using Facts You Know" Spinners (page 88)
- Deck of Number Cards 0–10 (page 107)
- Multiplication Chart (facedown, except when used to check products) (page 108)
- Game Rules, if needed, after presentation (page 125)

Object: Players multiply their "spinner number" by the number on their card. Larger (or smaller) product wins.

How to Play:

1. Each player:
   - Spins for his/her "spinner number."
   - Draws a number card from the deck.
   - Multiplies the "spinner number" by the number on his/her card.
   - Says the equation (for example, "7 times 4 equals 28").

2. The player with the larger product wins both cards.

3. Repeat until the deck is used up. The player with the most cards wins.

4. Shuffle the cards and play again.
   Smaller product wins.

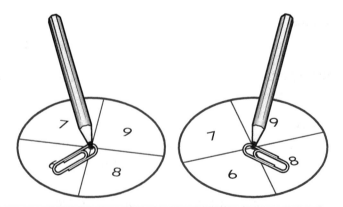

Variations

- Flip a coin to determine the winner (heads: larger product; tails: smaller product).
- Use the Alternate Spinner (multiples of 3, 4, 9, and 6) (page 87).

Explaining the Game: Using Facts You Know – Four in a Row

Number of Players: 2

Materials:

For each pair of students:

- "Using Facts You Know – Four in a Row" Game Board A (page 89)
- 4 sets of Number Cards 6, 7, 8, and 9 (page 107)
- Tiles or other markers
- "Using Facts You Know" Game Board B (optional, page 90)
- Game Rules, if needed, after presentation (page 126)

Object: Multiply to capture four adjacent numbers in a row (horizontal, vertical, or diagonal).

How to Play:

1. Players take turns drawing a card.

2. The player whose turn it is:
   - Multiplies the number on the card by one of the factors at the top of the page.
   - Says the multiplication fact and places a tile on the product.

3. If that product has already been captured, it is the other player's turn.

4. The first player to capture four adjacent numbers in a row wins.

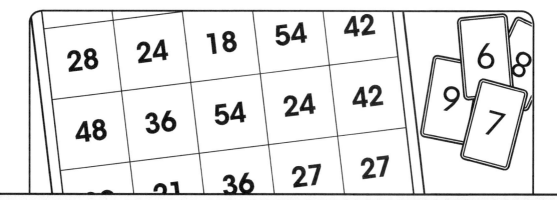

Variations

- Play cooperatively:
  - Capture all the numbers that outline the board. Avoid capturing other numbers.
  - Play "blackout:" capture all the numbers on the board.

Differentiation

Warm-Up B

More Support

- Provide 1-cm graph paper for students to sketch additional area models such as 8 × 4 and 7 × 3. Have students label the dimensions to figure out how many tiles are in each area model by using a chunking method.

"Using Facts You Know" Game

More Support

- Initially limit the number cards to 0–5 when playing this game. Then gradually add the other number cards to the deck.

"Using Facts You Know – Four in a Row" Game

More Support

- Play cooperatively. Goal could be to get five in a row, outline the board, or capture every square (blackout).

More Challenge

- Create a game board for the factors 6, 7, 8, and 9, and the cards 6, 7, 8, and 9. Play the game.

Deepening the Understanding

Ask the class:	Mathematical Practices (CCSSM)
Ali says that 8 × 9 is the same as doubling 4 × 9. Maddy says that 8 × 9 is the same as 8 × 5 and 8 × 4. Who is right? Why? Do you agree or disagree? Why?	MP2 Reason abstractly and quantitatively. MP3 Construct viable arguments and critique the reasoning of others. MP7 Look for and make use of structure. MP8 Look for and express regularity in repeated reasoning.
(Show a multiplication chart.) The "doubles" strategy works when thinking about: • 2s and 4s • 3s and 6s • 4s and 8s What do you notice about these pairs of fact families? Why do you think the "doubles" strategy works? Do you agree or disagree? Why?	MP2 Reason abstractly and quantitatively. MP3 Construct viable arguments and critique the reasoning of others. MP7 Look for and make use of structure. MP8 Look for and express regularity in repeated reasoning.

Putting It All Together

Learning Objectives

Fluently multiply numbers by each of the factors, 0–10. Students may use properties of operations to multiply.

Content Standard

Fluently multiply . . . within 100, using strategies such as the relationship between multiplication and division . . . or properties of operations. By the end of Grade 3, know from memory all products of two one-digit numbers. (CCSSM: 3.OA.7)

Prerequisite Skills

- Students should have strategies for multiplying all facts within 100, but may not yet have automaticity for all facts. (Units 3-1, 3-2, 3-3, and 3-4)
- Students should also have strategies for fluently adding and subtracting one- and two-digit numbers within 100.

General Vocabulary

English	Spanish
unique numbers	*números únicos*

Materials

For each pair of students:	Warm-Up A	Warm-Up B	"Putting It All Together" Game
• Deck of Number Cards 2–10 (page 107)	✓	✓	✓
• Game Board A (page 91)	✓		✓
• Game Board B (optional, page 92)			✓
• Coin to flip	✓	✓	
• Colored markers			✓

4	6	8	10	12	14	16	18	20
6	9	12	15	18	21	24	27	30
8	12	16	20	24	28	32	36	40
10	15	20	25	30	35	40	45	50
12	18	24	30	36	42	48	54	60
14	21	28	35	42	49	56	63	70

Warm-Up A: Lucky Squares

Materials:

- Deck of Number Cards 2–10 (page 107)
- Coin to flip

Directions:

1. Players turn one card faceup for the first factor.

2. Each player draws another card for the other factor and multiplies.

3. Players flip a coin to determine the goal (heads: larger product; tails: smaller product).

4. Winner collects all three cards. Exceptions:

   (a) If anyone has a square product, s/he wins.

   (b) For ties, each player draws another card and multiplies. The winner takes all.

5. The game is over when the deck is used up. The winner has the most cards.

Warm-Up B: Multiplication War

Materials:

- Deck of Number Cards 2–10 (page 107)
- Coin to flip

Object: Collect the most cards by multiplying two numbers.

Directions:

1. Each player turns over two number cards and multiplies.

2. Flip a coin to determine the target of the round (heads: larger product; tails: smaller product).

3. The winner takes all four cards. In the case of a tie, deal four more cards and winner takes all.

Explaining the Game: Putting It All Together

Number of Players: 2

Materials:

For each pair of students:

- "Putting It All Together" Game Board A (page 91)
- Deck of Number Cards 2–10 (page 107)
- Colored pencils or markers
- "Putting It All Together" Game Board B (optional, page 92)
- Game Rules, if needed, after presentation (page 127)

Object: Multiply two numbers to "capture" a number on the game board. The first player to capture three sets of three adjacent numbers in a row (horizontal, vertical, or diagonal) wins.

How to Play:

1. Deal five cards to each player.

2. Taking turns, players:

   (a) Multiply two of the cards together to "capture" a number on the game board.

   (b) Mark that square with "your" color, and discard those two cards.

   (c) Draw two new cards.

3. Instead of capturing a number, the player whose turn it is may discard all five cards and draw new cards. Then that player's turn is over.

4. The first player to capture three sets of three numbers in a row wins.

4	6	8	10	12	14	16	18	20
6	9	12	15	18	21	24	27	30
8	12	16	20	24	28	32	36	40
10	15	20	25	30	35	40	45	50
12	18	24	30	36	42	48	54	60
14	21	28	35	42	49	56	63	70
16	24	32	40	48	56	64	72	80
18	27	36	45	54	63	72	81	90
20	30	40	50	60	70	80	90	100

The player marking with circles wins. Notice that a player may use a captured number as part of more than one set of three numbers.

(*Note:* To have a record of play, have students record each equation.)

Differentiation

Warm-Up B: "Multiplication War"

More Support

- Begin by targeting one factor for each game. Turn over the "target factor" card—for example, 4.

- Allow the use of a multiplication chart (page 108).

"Putting It All Together" Game

More Support

- Play cooperatively. Work together to get three sets of five in a row.

More Challenge

- Game Board B has numbers in random order for additional challenge.

Deepening the Understanding

Ask the class:	Mathematical Practices (CCSSM)
What is special about Game Board A? (It is a multiplication chart.)	MP2 Reason abstractly and quantitatively.
Examine the board (or cut it apart) to answer these questions:	MP7 Look for and make use of structure.
• How many unique numbers are in the chart?	
• What is/are the most-repeated number(s)? Why?	
• Which numbers appear only once? Why?	
Find the even and odd numbers on the chart. Are they equally represented? Why?	

Is That a Fact?

Learning Objectives

Quickly name a missing factor or quotient.

Content Standard

Understand division as an unknown-factor problem. (CCSSM: 3.OA.6)

Prerequisite Skills

Students should:

- Understand the operation of subtraction; being fluent to 100 is helpful.

- Understand how to read and write division operation signs.

- Have strategies for multiplying all facts within 100, but not necessarily have automaticity for all facts. (Games 3-1, 3-2, 3-3, and 3-4)

- Be familiar with +/– fact families (understand related operations).

Math Vocabulary

dividend	product
divisor	quotient
factor	

Materials

For each pair of students:	Warm-Up A	Warm-Up B	"Is That a Fact?" Game
• Deck of Number Cards 0–10 (page 107)	✓	✓	✓
• Deck of Product/Dividend Cards (pages 109–110)	✓		
• Multiplication Chart (page 108)			✓

Warm-Up A: All in the Family

Number of Players: 2

Materials:

- Deck (4 sets) of Number Cards 6–9, called "factor cards" in this game (page 107)
- Deck (one set) of Product/Dividend Cards, called "product cards" in this game (pages 109–110)

  (*Note:* These Product/Dividend Cards are used again in Game 3-7.)

Object: Win cards by making multiplication/division fact families.

Directions:

1. Deal five factor cards to each player. Put four product cards on the table.

2. Taking turns, players:
   - Use two factor cards from their hand and one product card to create a multiplication fact.
   - Move the same three cards around to make a division fact.
   - Put those three cards in the player's "win" pile.
   - Draw two more factor cards and put a new product card on the table. Then the player's turn is over.

3. If a player cannot play, he/she replaces a factor card or a product card. The player's turn is over.

4. The winner has the most "win" pile cards when the factor deck is gone.

Variations

- Students play cooperatively by putting all cards in a common "win pile."
- "Square Number" variation: If a product card is a square number, say the multiplication fact and win that card. Draw another product card and continue your turn.

Warm-Up B: Secret Number

Number of Players: 2

Materials:

- Deck of Number Cards 0–10 (page 107)

Object: Win cards by figuring out the secret number.

Directions:

1. Players take turns. Player 1:
   - Draws one card from deck and places it faceup on the table.
   - Draws another card and keeps it a secret in his/her hand.
   - Announces the product of the two cards.

2. Player 2 figures out the "secret number" by thinking about the missing factor or dividing.

⬤ Explaining the Game: Is That a Fact?

Number of Players: 3 (1 captain; 2 crewmembers)

Materials:

For each team of three:

- Deck of Number Cards 0–9 (page 107)
- Multiplication Chart (page 108) for the captain to use, if needed (otherwise, kept facedown)
- Paper and pencil
- Game Rules, if needed, after presentation (page 128)

Object: Figure out the unseen number on your forehead while seeing your partner's number and the product of the two numbers.

How to Play:

1. The captain says "salute," and each crewmember puts a card on his/her forehead.

2. The captain says and writes the product.

3. The cards stay on crewmembers' foreheads until each crewmember has figured out his/her own number.

4. The first crewmember to correctly say his/her own number wins one point.

Differentiation

More Support

- Being the "captain" is typically a more straightforward role. If students need more support, start them in this role for a couple of rounds. Supply a multiplication chart for the captain to use for checking.

- Play a cooperative version of the game:

  ~ The captain is the timer. He/she calls time after 15–20 seconds and then asks for solutions.

  ~ Each crewmember explains how he/she figured out the solution.

  ~ Each player wins a point if he/she is correct.

More Challenge

- Have the captain announce the decade range of the product rather than the actual product.

  For example, the captain says, "In the 40s." Crewmember 1 thinks, "I see my partner has 9, so I know my card must be 5. The product is 45." In some cases there will be more than one correct factor, and the player must keep listing them until he gets the correct one. For instance, if the captain says, "In the 30s," crewmember 1 thinks, "My partner's card is 6, so my card could be 5 or 6."

Deepening the Understanding

Ask the class:	Mathematical Practices (CCSSM)
Jon's captain said the product was 42. He could see a "6" card on his partner's forehead. What are some ways Jon could figure out his number?	MP2 Reason abstractly and quantitatively.
Maria's captain said the product was 24. She could see a "3" card on her partner's forehead. 1. Use the words *product* and *factor* to describe this scenario. 2. Use the words *dividend, divisor,* and *quotient* to describe this situation. Which way of thinking about this problem (multiplication or division) matches your strategy?	MP2 Reason abstractly and quantitatively.
What are the related division facts for 6 × 8 = 48? For 5 × 7 = 35? How can you make a related division fact for any multiplication statement?	MP2 Reason abstractly and quantitatively.

Let's Divvy It Up

Learning Objectives

Fluently divide within 100, using strategies such as the relationship between multiplication and division or properties of operations.

Content Standard

Fluently . . . divide within 100, using strategies such as the relationship between multiplication and division . . . or properties of operations. By the end of Grade 3, know from memory all products of two one-digit numbers. (CCSSM: 3.OA.7)

Prerequisite Skills

Students should have strategies for multiplying all facts within 100, but may not yet have automaticity for all facts.

Math Vocabulary

dividend

divisor

quotient

Materials

For each pair of students:	Warm-Up	"Let's Divvy It Up" Game
• "Divide By . . ." Spinners A, B, & C (pages 93–97)	✓	
• Multiplication Chart (page 108)	✓	
• Deck of Number Cards 2–9 (page 107)		✓
• Product/Dividend Cards (pages 109–110)		✓
• Game Board (page 98)		✓

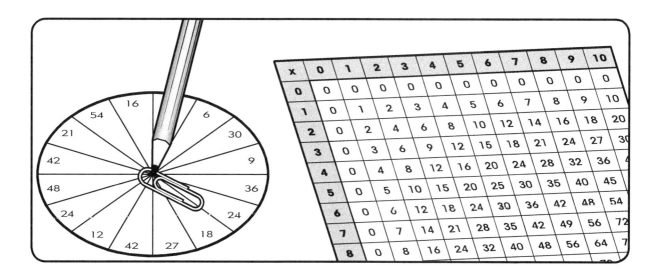

Warm-Up: Divide By . . .

Number of Players: 2

Materials:

For each pair of students:
- "Divide by …" Spinners A, B, and C (pages 93–97)
- Multiplication Chart (page 108)

Object: Get 16 or more quotients right out of 20 spins for each spinner.

Directions:

1. Pick a spinner. (Teacher assigns or students choose.)

2. Spin for the dividend.

3. Divide by the divisor for that spinner.

4. Each player writes the quotient.

5. Players compare their quotients. Check using the multiplication chart, if needed. If both are correct, circle the quotient.

6. Spin again. Do 20 spins. If players get 16 correct out of 20, it's time for a new spinner.

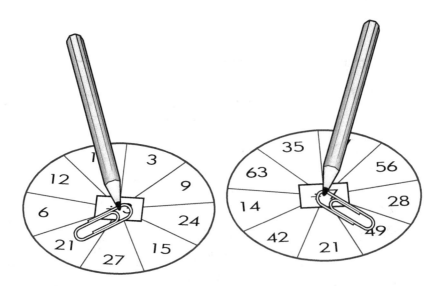

◯ Explaining the Game: Let's Divvy It Up

Number of Players: 2

Materials:

For each pair of students:

- Deck of Number Cards 2–9 (remove the 5), called "divisor cards" (page 107)
- Deck of Product/Dividend Cards, called "dividend cards" (pages 109–110)
- Game Board (page 98)
- Game Rules, if needed, after presentation (page 129)

Object: Collect the most dividend cards by correctly dividing.

How to Play:

1. Place the divisor and dividend card decks on the game board. Place one divisor card faceup.

2. Players take turns dividing the dividend by the divisor, if possible.

3. If the cards can be used to make a division fact (for example, 42 and 6), the player says the fact: "42 divided by 6 equals 7." If correct, the player puts the dividend card in his/her "win pile." Then it is the other player's turn.

4. If the cards cannot be used to make a division fact, the player whose turn it is draws a new divisor card and divides. If the new card cannot be used, the player's turn is over.

5. Play continues until all the dividend cards are used. The winner is the player with the most cards.

Variation

- The same rules as "Let's Divvy It Up," except: A player may collect any dividend card that is a square number at the beginning of his/her turn, even if s/he does not have the divisor card. The player just has to correctly identify its factors. Then that player also takes his/her turn dividing the dividend by the divisor, if possible.

Differentiation

Warm-Up: "Divide By ..."

More Challenge
(Above grade level)

- Play a divide-with-remainders version: Pick any spinner. Use the divisor cards 2–9. Spin for the dividend. Turn over a card for the divisor. What is the quotient? Is there a remainder?

"Let's Divvy It Up" Game

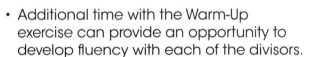

More Support

- Additional time with the Warm-Up exercise can provide an opportunity to develop fluency with each of the divisors.

- Begin by using just the Product/Dividend Cards 12, 14, 16, 18, 21, 24, 27, 28, 32, and 36.

- Have the Multiplication Chart available face down to check answers as needed.

 # Deepening the Understanding

Ask the class:	Mathematical Practices (CCSSM)
Is it possible to:	MP2 Reason abstractly and quantitatively.
• Evenly share an odd number of items with an even number of people?	MP3 Construct viable arguments and critique the reasoning of others.
• Evenly share an even number of items with an odd number of people?	
• Evenly share an odd number of items with an odd number of people?	
• Evenly share an even number of items with an even number of people?	
• Put an odd number of items evenly into an odd number of groups (for example, 25 items into 5 or 7 groups)? (Sometimes it is; sometimes it isn't.)	
Give examples for each.	
Do you agree or disagree? Why?	

For a dividend of 24, what are possible divisor/quotient pairs?	MP2 Reason abstractly and quantitatively.
What are other dividends in the multiplication chart that have more than one divisor/quotient pair?	MP3 Construct viable arguments and critique the reasoning of others.

Let's Get A-Round to It

Learning Objectives

Use place value understanding to round numbers to the nearest 10 or 100.

Content Standard

Use place value understanding to round numbers to the nearest 10 or 100. (CCSSM: 3.NBT.1)

Prerequisite Skills

Students need basic place value understanding of tens and ones.

Math Vocabulary

hundreds

round

tens

Materials

For each pair of students:	Warm-Ups	"Let's Get A-Round to It" Game
• Deck of Number Cards 0–9 (page 107)	✓	✓
• Table for Listing Rounded Numbers (page 99)	✓	
• Game Boards A–C (pages 100–101)		✓
• Colored markers		✓
For the class:		
• 32 large (8 × 5-in. or 4 × 6-in.) index cards	✓	

10	20	30	40	50	60	70	80	90	100
110	120	130	140	150	160	170	180	190	200
210	220	230	240	250	260	270	280	290	300
310	320	330	340	350	360	370	380	390	400
410	420	430	440	450	460	470	480	490	500
510	520	530	540	550	560	570	580	590	60
610	620	630	640	650	660	670	680	690	7
710	720	730	740	750	760	770	780	790	

Warm-Up A: The Nearest . . .

Number of Players: 2

Materials:

- Deck of Number Cards 0–9 (page 107)
- One class set of 32 large index cards with one of these numbers on each:

  Set A: 0, 10, 20, 30, 40, 50, 60, 70, 80, 90, 100

  Set B: 100, 200, 300, 400, 500, 600, 700, 800, 900, 1000

  Set C: 300, 310, 320, 330, 340, 350, 360, 370, 380, 390, 400

Object: Get 16 or more quotients right out of 20 spins for each spinner.

Directions:

Part 1: The Nearest Ten

1. Make a large number line by posting the Set A numbers across the front of the room.

2. Have students take turns drawing two Number Cards (0–9) to make a two-digit number to display on a projector. Zero may not be used as the leading digit.

3. Call on a student to write that number on a paper and stand in front of the number line at the "nearest ten" holding that number.

4. Ask the class if they agree or not, and why.

5. Repeat with other numbers.

Part 2: The Nearest Hundred

6. Next, replace the Set A numbers with the Set B numbers. Have students draw three Number Cards to make a three-digit number.

7. Repeat the process above, rounding to the nearest hundred.

Part 3: The Nearest Ten with Three-Digit Numbers

8. Finally, replace the Set B numbers with the Set C numbers. Have students put a "3" Number Card in the hundreds place and then draw two more cards to make a three-digit number.

9. Repeat the process above, rounding to the nearest ten.

Warm-Up B: Three-Digit Rounding

Number of Players: 2

Materials:

- Deck of Number Cards 0–9 (page 107) for each pair of students
- Table for Listing Rounded Numbers (page 99) for each student.

Directions:

1. Work cooperatively with a partner.
2. Draw three numbers.
3. On the Table for Listing Rounded Numbers, each partner records all the possible numbers that can be made with those three digits, from the smallest to the largest. (Zero may not be used as the leading digit.)
4. Round each number to the nearest hundred and record in the table.

Example: Table for Listing Rounded Numbers (the three cards you drew: 3, 6, and 7)

All the Possible 3-Digit Numbers	Round to the Nearest 100	Round to the Nearest 10
367	400	
376	400	
637	600	
673	700	
736	700	
763	800	

5. Then cover up the "Round to the Nearest Hundred" column and round the same numbers to the nearest ten.

Example: Table for Listing Rounded Numbers (the three cards you drew: 3, 6, and 7)

All the Possible 3-Digit Numbers	Round to the Nearest 100	Round to the Nearest 10
367		370
376		380
637		640
673		670
736		740
763		760

6. Draw three new cards and repeat.

Explaining the Game: Let's Get A-Round to It

Number of Players: 2

Materials:

For each pair of students:

- "Let's Get A-Round to It" Game Board A (page 100)
- Deck of Number Cards 0–9 (page 107)
- Colored pencils or markers
- Game Boards B and C (optional, page 100) – *See Differentiation section*
- Game Rules, if needed, after presentation (page 130)

Object: Round three-digit numbers to the nearest 10 or nearest 100 to capture three sets of three numbers in a row (horizontal, vertical, or diagonal).

How to Play:

1. Taking turns, players:

   - Draw four cards.

   - Select three of those cards to create a three-digit number. (Zero may be the leading digit.)

   - Round the number to the nearest 10 or nearest 100. Mark (capture) the number on the game board.

   - Discard all four cards.

2. The first player to capture three sets of three numbers in a row wins.

10	20	30	40	50	60	70	80	90	100
110	120	130	140	150	160	170	180	190	200
210	220	230	240	250	260	270	280	290	300
310	320	330	340	350	360	370	380	390	400
410	420	430	440	450	460	470	480	490	500
510	520	530	540	550	560	570	580	590	600
610	620	630	640	650	660	670	680	690	700
710	720	730	740	750	760	77	780	790	800
810	820	830	840	850	860	870		890	900
910	920	930	940	950	960	970	9	990	1000

The player marking with circles wins. Notice that a player may use a number as part of more than one set of three captured numbers.

 Differentiation

"Let's Get A-Round to It" Game

More Support

- Begin by using Game Board B:
  - ~ Draw three cards.
  - ~ Make a two-digit number; discard the extra card.
  - ~ Round to the nearest 10.
- Use Game Board C. Draw three cards. Round to the nearest hundred.

Deepening the Understanding

Ask the class:	Mathematical Practices (CCSSM)	
If you had the cards 3, 6, and 7, and the game is to round to the nearest hundred, what are all the numbers you could capture? If you had the cards 3, 6, and 7, and the game is to round to the nearest ten, what are all the numbers could you capture?	MP2	Reason abstractly and quantitatively.
What are all the numbers that would be 590 when rounded to the nearest 10? Show these on a number line. What are all the numbers that would be 700 when rounded to the nearest hundred? How many different numbers are there that would round to any nearest ten, such as 640? How many different numbers are there that would round to any nearest hundred, such as 600? Why? Ask the class if they agree or disagree and why. Ask students to give examples to support their opinions.	MP2	Reason abstractly and quantitatively.
	MP3	Construct viable arguments and critique the reasoning of others.
	MP7	Look for and make use of structure.
	MP8	Look for and express regularity in repeated reasoning.

The Multiples of 10

Learning Objectives

Multiply one-digit whole numbers by multiples of 10.

Content Standards

Multiply one-digit whole numbers by multiples of 10 in the range of 10–90 (e.g., 9 × 80, 5 × 60) using strategies based on place value and properties of operations. (CCSSM: 3.NBT.3)

Fluently multiply . . . within 100, using strategies such as the relationship between multiplication and division . . . or properties of operations. By the end of Grade 3, know from memory all products of two one-digit numbers. (CCSSM: 3.OA.7)

Prerequisite Skills

Students should have strategies for multiplying all facts within 100, but may not yet have automaticity for all facts.

Math Vocabulary

multiple

Materials

For each pair of students:	Warm-Up	"Multiples of 10" Game
• Deck of Number Cards 0–9 (page 107)	✓	✓
• Game Board (page 102)		✓
• Index card	✓	✓
• Colored markers		✓

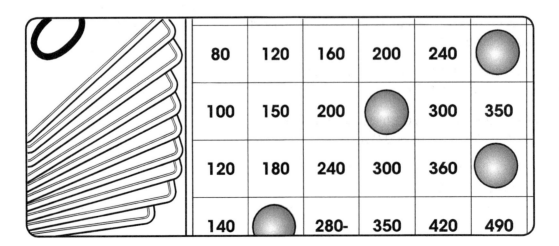

Warm-Up: Zero In on Multiples of 10

Number of Players: 2

Materials:

For each pair of students:

- Deck of Number Cards 0–9 (page 107) – remove the 0.

- Index card (write "× 10" on one side of the card and "0" on the reverse)

Object: Take turns saying a multiplication fact or its multiple of 10.

Directions:

1. Student 1 draws two number cards (for example, 6 and 7) and says, "6 × 7 = 42."

2. Student 2: Places the "× 10" index card next to one of the cards (for example, "6"). The student then flips the card to make 60 (because 6 × 10 = 60) and says, "60 × 7 = 420."

3. Alternate which student starts.

Explaining the Game: The Multiples of 10

Number of Players: 2

Materials:

For each pair of students:

- "The Multiples of 10" Game Board (page 102)
- Deck of Number Cards 2–9 (page 107)
- Game Rules, if needed, after presentation (page 131)
- "× 10" index card (from the Warm-Up exercise)
- Colored markers

Object: Multiply a one-digit number by a multiple of 10 to capture three sets of three adjacent numbers in a row (horizontal, vertical, or diagonal).

40	60	80	100	120	140	160	180	200
60	90	120	150	180	210	240	270	300
80	120	160	200	240	280	320	360	400
100	150	200	250	300	350	400	450	500
120	180	240	300	360	420	480	540	600
140	210	280	350	420	490	560	630	700
160	240	320	400	480	560	640	720	800
180	270	360	450	540	630	720	810	900
200	300	400	500	600	700	800	900	1000

The player marking with rectangles wins. Notice that a player may use a number as part of more than one set of three captured products.

How to Play:

1. Dealer deals five cards to each player. Taking turns, players:

   - Choose two cards and use the "× 10" card to create a multiplication expression. Say the expression (for example, "4 × 80") and solve it.

   - Mark ("capture") the product on the board.

   - Discard the two number cards and draw two new cards.

2. The first player to capture three sets of three numbers in a row wins.

Differentiation

More Support

- Play cooperatively. Work together to get three sets of five in a row.

More Challenge (Above grade level)

- Play the game with number cards 2–10.

Deepening the Understanding

Ask the class:	Mathematical Practices (CCSSM)
What is a quick way to multiply: $3 \times 60 = ?$ $4 \times 30 = ?$ $60 \times 7 = ?$ What "rule" or strategy works best for you?	MP2 Reason abstractly and quantitatively.
Andrew says this is a true statement: $80 \times 3 = 30 \times 8$. Do you agree or disagree? Why?	MP2 Reason abstractly and quantitatively. MP3 Construct viable arguments and critique the reasoning of others.

That's "Sum" Difference

Learning Objectives

Fluently add and subtract three-digit whole numbers using algorithms with a special focus on place value.

Content Standard

Fluently add and subtract within 1000 using strategies and algorithms based on place value ... (CCSSM: 3.NBT.2)

Prerequisite Skills

Students should be:

- Nearly fluent with adding and subtracting within 100.

- Able to use algorithms to add and subtract multi-digit numbers.

Math Vocabulary

algorithm

Materials

For each pair of students:

- Deck of 100, 10, and 1 cards (page 103)

- Deck of Number Cards 0–9 (page 107)

- Spinner (page 104)

- Chips (small counters)

	Warm-Ups	"That's 'Sum' Difference" Game
	✓	
		✓
		✓
		✓

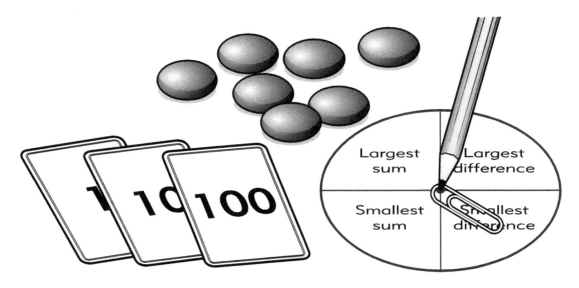

Warm-Up: Addition Version – Race to 1,000

Number of Players: 2–3

Materials:

For each group:

- Deck of 100, 10, and 1 Cards – 12 of each card (page 103)

Object: Add three-digit numbers. Be the first to have a sum over 1,000.

Directions:

Taking turns, players:

1. Draw five cards and write the sum. Discard those cards.

2. After the first turn, add the sum of the five cards to the previous sum.

3. Shuffle and reuse the discard deck as needed.

4. Continue playing until one player's sum is over 1,000.

Variation for Subtraction: Race Back to 300

Object: Be the first player to have a difference that is less than 300.

Use the same materials and rules as for "Race to 1000" except:

- In Step 1, subtract the first sum from 1,000.
- In Step 2, subtract the sum from the previous difference.

Explaining the Game: That's "Sum" Difference

Number of Players: 2

Materials:

- Deck of Number Cards 0–9 (page 107)
- Spinner (page 104)
- Game Rules, if needed, after presentation (page 132)
- Chips or counters
- Student-made double place value mats
  (Fold 11 × 17-in. paper into thirds and cut in half—"hotdog fold"—for two mats.)

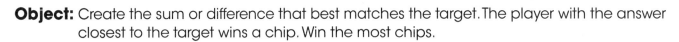

Object: Create the sum or difference that best matches the target. The player with the answer closest to the target wins a chip. Win the most chips.

How to Play:

1. A player spins to determine the target of the game.

2. Taking turns, players draw and place one card at a time in a different position on the place value mat to make a three-digit number. Once a card is placed, it can't be moved. Do not use zero in the hundreds place.

2. Players draw a fourth card. Use it to replace one of the cards, or discard it.

3. Players repeat steps 1 and 2 to make the second three-digit number.

4. Finally, players add or subtract the two numbers according to the spinner target and record their work.

5. The player with the closest sum or difference to the target wins a chip.

(*Note:* Remind players to subtract the smaller number from the larger number when subtracting.)

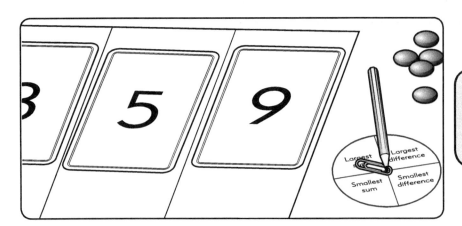

To use the spinner, place a pencil tip through a paper clip.

Differentiation

Warm-Ups

More Support

- Players can do the calculating one card at a time. For example, a player has 312 and on the next turn draws 100, 10, 10, 1, and 1.

For the Addition Version, players can add like this:

312 + 100 = 412;

412 + 10 = 422; etc.

Or take the next step:

Combine by place value and then add in stages like this:

312 + 100 = 412;

412 + 20 = 432;

432 + 2 = 434

For the Subtraction Variation, players can subtract like this:

312 – 100 = 212;

212 – 10 = 202; etc.

Or combine by place value and then subtract in stages.

"That's 'Sum' Difference" Game

More Support

- Start with two-digit numbers. Use alternative algorithms such as partial sum/difference. For example, to add 47 + 98:

40 + 90 = 130 (first partial sum, adding the tens)

7 + 8 = 15 (other partial sum, adding the ones)

130
+15
~~145~~ (sum)

More Challenge

- Draw three cards to make a three-digit number. That is the target number.

- Create two three-digit numbers (steps 1–2 of the game).

- Each player may choose to add or subtract to get as close as possible to the target number.

Deepening the Understanding

Ask the class:	Mathematical Practices (CCSSM)
When the target is to form the largest sum, what is: ...a general strategy for placing the number cards? ...the largest difference? ...the smallest sum? ...the smallest difference?	MP2 Reason abstractly and quantitatively. MP8 Look for and express regularity in repeated reasoning.
If you create two five-digit numbers by using each of the 0–9 Number Cards only once and not using zero as the leading digit: • What is the largest possible sum? • What is the smallest possible sum? • What is the largest possible difference? • What is the smallest possible difference? Explain how you know.	MP2 Reason abstractly and quantitatively. MP7 Look for and make use of structure.
Note: After a student shares an idea, ask the class if they agree or disagree. Why? Why not?	MP3 Construct viable arguments and critique the reasoning of others.

Match the Fractions

Learning Objectives

Recognize equivalent fractions among halves, 3rds, 4ths, 6ths, and 8ths, and equivalents to whole numbers 0 and 1.

Content Standards

Understand two fractions as equivalent (equal) if they are the same size, or the same point on a number line. (CCSSM: 3.NF.3.a)

Recognize . . . simple equivalent fractions, e.g., 1/2 = 2/4, 4/6 = 2/3. Explain why the fractions are equivalent. (CCSSM: 3.NF.3.b)

Express whole numbers as fractions, and recognize fractions that are equivalent to whole numbers. (CCSSM: 3.NF.3.c)

(*Note:* Only the whole numbers 0 and 1 are represented as fractions in this unit.)

Prerequisite Skills

Some familiarity with matching pictorial representations of fractions with numerical representations of fractions will be helpful.

Math Vocabulary

equivalent

Materials

For each pair of students:	Warm-Up	"Match the Fractions" Game
• Fraction Picture Cards (pages 117–121)	✓	
• Fraction Number Cards (pages 111–116)	✓	✓
• Fraction Notes (pages 105–106)	✓	

Warm-Up: Sorting Out Fractions

Number of Players: 2

Materials:

For each student:

- Fraction Notes (pages 105–106)

For each pair:

- Mixed deck of both Fraction Number and Fraction Picture Cards (pages 111–121) – include whole numbers 0 and 1, but remove wild cards.

Directions:

1. Introduce the fraction cards. Show area model cards and number line cards for 1/4 and 2/6. Ask students how the models represent those fractions.

2. Have students:

- Match the Fraction Picture Cards to the Fraction Number Cards that show the same value.

- Arrange the cards into groups of equivalent fractions.

- Complete the Fraction Notes (pages 105–106).

(*Note:* When finished, have students set aside the Fraction Number Cards that have no equivalent fractions in this set (1/6, 5/6, 1/8, 3/8, 5/8, 7/8). Those cards are not used again in this unit.)

Explaining the Game: Match the Fractions

Number of Players: 2

Materials:

For each pair of students:

- Deck of Fraction Number Cards (page 111–113) and whole numbers 0 and 1 (Remove 1/6, 5/6, 1/8, 3/8, 5/8, 7/8.)
- Game Rules, if needed, after presentation (page 133)
- Completed Fraction Notes pages (optional) – for reference

Object: Collect pairs of equivalent fractions.

How to Play:

1. Dealer deals three cards to each player.

1. Taking turns, players draw one or more cards from the deck until they can make an equivalent pair. The player whose turn it is says the equation (for example, 1/2 = 2/4) and puts the cards in his/her win pile.

2. Play continues until one player goes out or the deck is used up.

3. Players subtract the number of cards still in their hands from the number of cards in their win piles for their final scores.

Wild Card Variation

- Include two or three wild cards. Players tell which fraction a wild card represents.

Differentiation

"Match the Fraction" Game

More Support

- Begin by playing the game with only the Fraction Picture Cards. Then switch to using the Fraction Number Cards.

- Begin by limiting the deck to halves, 4ths, and 8ths.

More Challenge (Above grade level)

- Have students create additional fraction cards (2/10, 4/10, 5/10, 6/10, 8/10, and 2/12, 3/12, 4/12, 6/12, 8/12, 9/12, and 10/12) and use them in the game.

Deepening the Understanding

Ask the class:	Mathematical Practices (CCSSM)	
Dale says: 3/4 and 6/8 name the same amount.	MP2	Reason abstractly and quantitatively.
Chip says: That's impossible. 6/8 is twice as much as 3/4.	MP3	Construct viable arguments and critique the reasoning of others.
Who is correct? Explain your thinking.		
Alana says that 1/4 of an hour and 4/12 of an hour are the same. Ben says they are not.	MP2	Reason abstractly and quantitatively.
Use a clock to show who is right.	MP3	Construct viable arguments and critique the reasoning of others.
Rudy says that 6/12 of a foot and 1/2 of a foot are not the same distance. Suzy says they are the same distance.	MP2	Reason abstractly and quantitatively.
Use a ruler to show who is right.	MP3	Construct viable arguments and critique the reasoning of others.

Wild Card Fractions

Learning Objectives

Recognize fractions. Compare two fractions when either the numerators or the denominators match.

Content Standard

Compare two fractions with the same numerator or the same denominator by reasoning about their size . . . Record the results of comparisons with the symbols >, =, or <, and justify the conclusions, e.g., by using a visual fraction model. (CCSSM: 3.NF.3.d)

Prerequisite Skills

Students should be able to recognize equivalent fractions (halves, thirds, fourths, sixths, eighths). (Game 3-11)

Math Vocabulary

denominator

numerator

Materials

For each pair of students:

	Warm-Ups	"Wild Card Fractions" Game
• Fraction Number Cards (pages 111–113)	✓	✓
• Fraction Picture Cards (pages 114–118)	✓	
• Coin to flip		✓
• Privacy barrier		✓

Warm-Up A: Sort by Denominator

Number of Players: 2

Materials:

For each pair of students:
- Deck of Fraction Number Cards (pages 111–116), with whole numbers 0 and 1 removed
- Deck of Fraction Picture Cards (pages 117–121), with whole numbers 0 and 1 removed
- 8 student-made small cards with ">" on one side (rotate for "<")

Directions:

Have students:

1. Organize the Fraction Number Cards into sets with the same denominator. Arrange the cards in each set from smallest to largest.

2. Put the ">" or "<" symbol card between each fraction.

3. Put a matching Fraction Picture Card below each Fraction Number Card.

4. Describe how the picture cards match the number cards.

 # Warm-Up B: Sort by Numerator

Number of Players: 2

Materials:

For each pair of students:
- Deck of Fraction Number Cards (pages 111–116), with whole numbers 0 and 1 removed
- Deck of Fraction Picture Cards (pages 117–121), with whole numbers 0 and 1 removed
- Seven student-made small cards with ">" on one side (rotate for "<")

Directions:

1. Organize the Fraction Number Cards into sets with the same numerator. Arrange the cards in each set from smallest to largest.

2. Put the ">" or "<" symbol card between each fraction.

3. Put a matching Fraction Picture Card below each Fraction Number Card.

Explaining the Game: Wild Card Fractions

Number of Players: 2

Materials:

- Deck of Fraction Number Cards (pages 111–116) and 6 wild cards
- Game Rules, if needed, after presentation (page 134)
- Coin
- Two privacy barriers
- Completed Fraction Notes pages from Game 3-11 (optional)

Object: Win the most cards by comparing fractions and explaining comparisons.

How to Play:

1. Each player draws five cards. Use privacy barriers. Players take turns going first.

2. Player 1 puts a card on the table. (Do not lead with a wild card.)

3. Player 2 matches either the numerator or denominator. A wild card may be used to represent a specific fraction.

4. If Player 2 has no card to play, s/he draws cards until s/he can play.

5. Players flip a coin (heads: greater fraction wins; tails: smaller fraction wins).

6. The winner explains the comparison and puts both cards in his/her "win pile." If the fractions are equivalent, play again. Winner takes all four cards.

7. Play continues until all cards are played or until a player is stuck. The winner has the most "win pile" cards.

Differentiation

More Support

- Use the completed Fraction Notes pages from Game 3-11 as a reference.

- Make a list of the fractions in order after doing Warm-Up 1 and Warm-Up 2. Then use these lists as references during the game.

- Students could take photos of the arrangements made in the Warm-Ups and use the photos as a reference.

More Challenge – Above grade level

- Use both Fraction Picture Cards and Fraction Number Cards. Create a large number line. Put "0" on the left and "1" on the right. Arrange all the cards from smallest to largest.

- Play "Battling Fractions" (above grade level)
  (a) Player 1 writes a fraction, using any numerator or denominator.
  (b) Player 2 writes a fraction with either the same numerator or the same denominator, but makes the other part of the fraction different.
  (c) Flip a coin to determine the target (< or >).

Deepening the Understanding

Ask the class:	Mathematical Practices (CCSSM)	
When comparing two fractions with the same denominator, how do you know which fraction is larger?	MP2	Reason abstractly and quantitatively.
How could you figure out which is larger, 5/12 or 7/12? Explain your thinking. Write a math sentence using the symbols < or >. (Use clock, egg carton, or logic.)	MP4	Model with Mathematics.
When comparing two fractions with the same numerator, how do you know which is larger?	MP2	Reason abstractly and quantitatively.
How could you figure out which is larger, 5/12 or 5/6? Explain your thinking. Write a math sentence using the symbols < or >. (Use clock, egg carton, or logic.)	MP4	Model with Mathematics.
How could you figure out which is larger, 7/8 or 7/16? Explain your thinking. Write a math sentence using the symbols < or >. (Use ruler, sketch, or logic.)	MP6	Attend to precision.
How could you figure out which is larger, 5/12 or 5/8? Explain your thinking. Write a math sentence using the symbols < or >. (Use logic.)		

Blackline Masters

ACTIVITY-SPECIFIC BLMs

BLMs USED IN MORE THAN ONE GAME

GAME RULES

"Double Trouble" Spinner (Game 3-1)

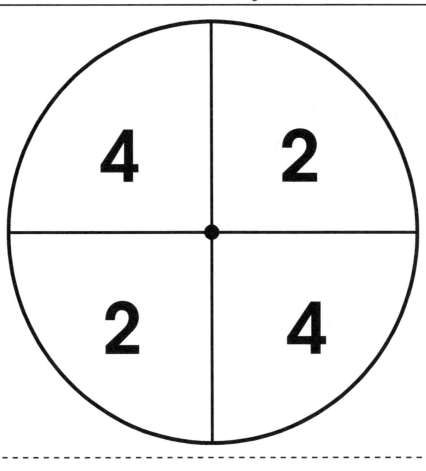

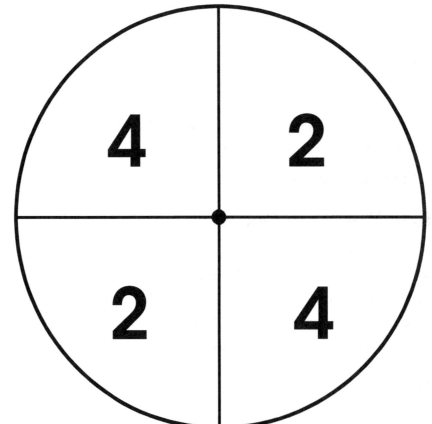

"Double Trouble – Four-in-a-Row"
Game Board (Game 3-1)

Use Number Cards:

Factors:

2	3	4	5	6	7	8	9

8	20	14	24	32
10	16	12	28	14
28	32	18	16	20
16	36	12	24	32
12	32	36	8	16

"Think About 10" Area Models (Game 3-2)

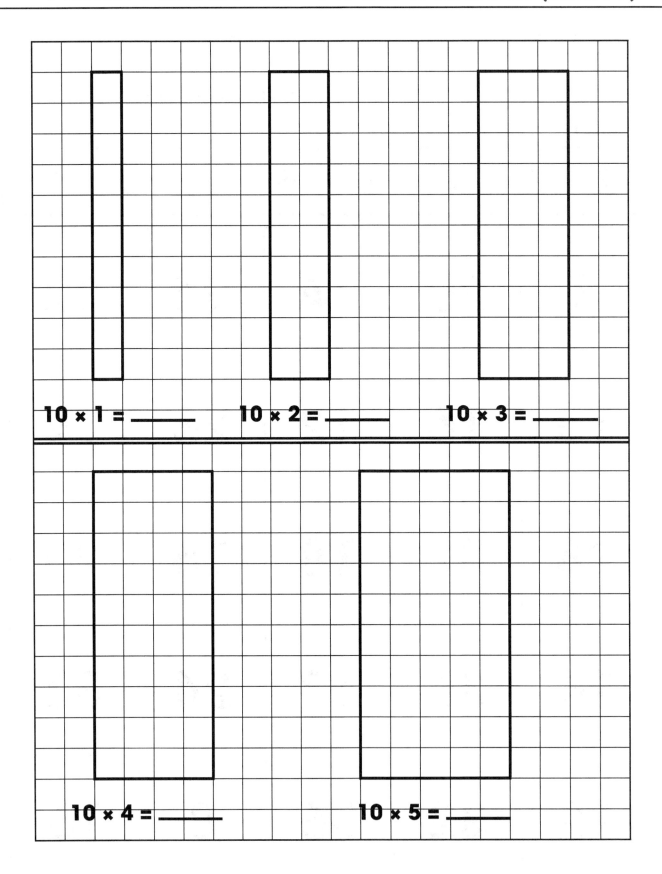

10 × 1 = _____   10 × 2 = _____   10 × 3 = _____

10 × 4 = _____   10 × 5 = _____

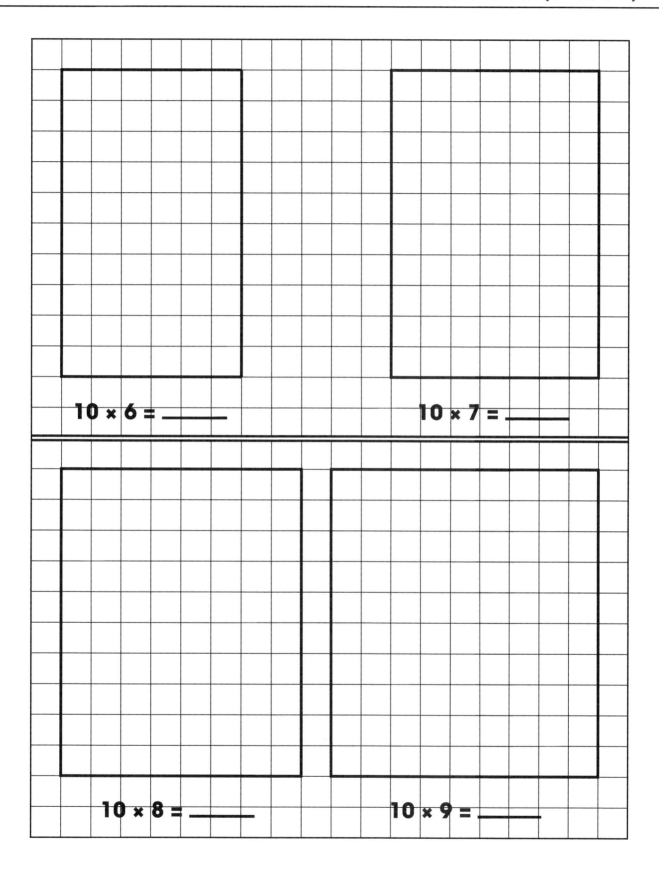

10 × 6 = _____

10 × 7 = _____

10 × 8 = _____

10 × 9 = _____

"Think About 10" Spinner (Game 3-2)

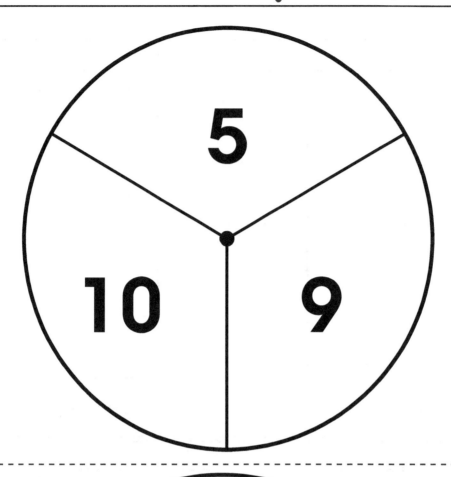

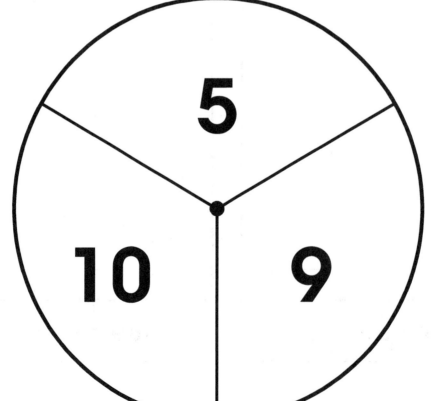

"Think About 10 – Four-in-a-Row"
Game Board A (Game 3-2)

Use Number Cards: 4 5 9 10

Factors:

1	2	3	4	5	6	7	8	9

9	20	40	27	63
28	15	18	25	90
32	72	54	45	30
54	24	36	36	35
81	18	63	35	72

"Think About 10 – Four-in-a-Row"
Game Board B (Game 3-2)

Use Number Cards: 2 5 9 10

Factors:

1	2	3	4	5	6
9	20	40	25	36
10	30	45	18	15
27	36	12	60	54
20	45	10	8	20
54	6	27	18	30

"Triple Trouble" Spinner (Game 3-3)

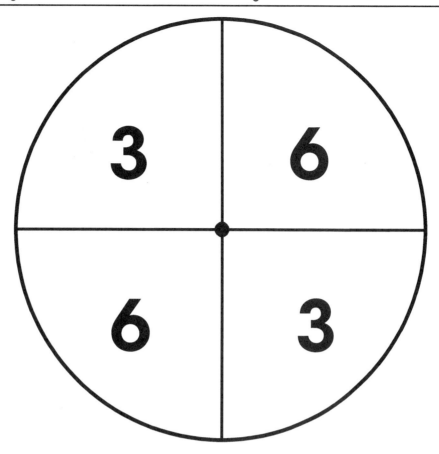

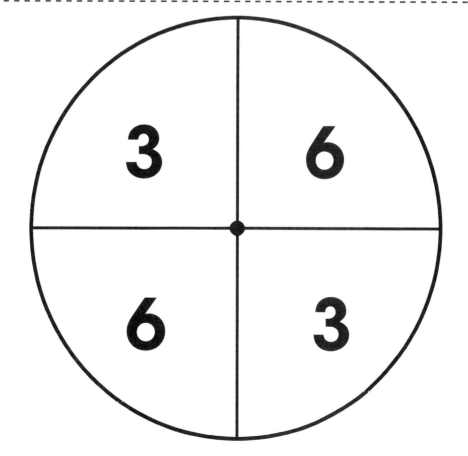

"Triple Trouble" Alternate Spinner (Game 3-3)

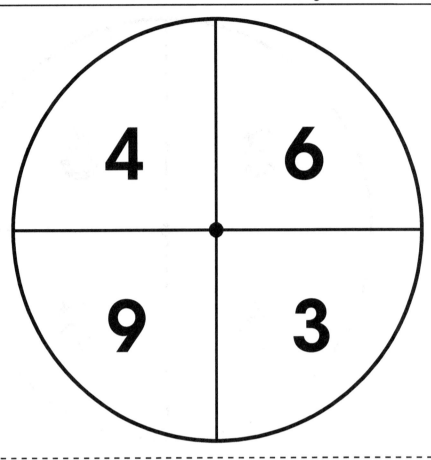

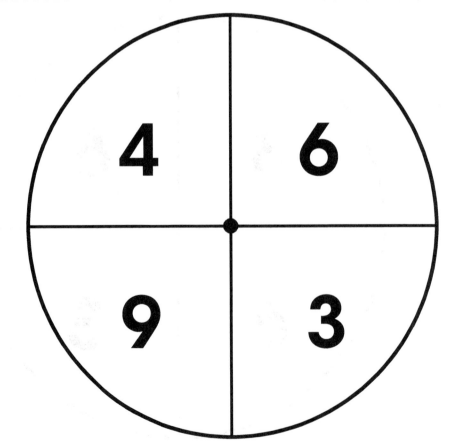

Use Number Cards: 3 4 6

Factors:

1	2	3	4	5	6	7	8	9

8	20	21	24	32
15	16	12	30	24
28	12	18	54	6
48	36	12	24	42
30	21	36	27	16

"Triple Trouble" Game Board B (Game 3-3)

Use Number Cards:

Factors:

2	3	4	5	6
36	35	21	24	32
15	16	12	45	24
28	24	18	54	42
48	36	54	24	42
30	21	36	27	27

"Triple Trouble" Game Board C (Game 3-3)

Use Number Cards: 3 4 6 9

Factors:

| 2 | 3 | 4 | 5 | 6 | 7 | 8 | 9 |

24	32	72	24	18
54	18	12	48	36
63	12	24	16	45
28	36	42	27	20
81	63	18	21	36

"Using Facts You Know"
Recording Sheet – page 1 (Game 3-4)

Label the dimensions. Draw a line to "chunk it" in an easy way. Show the partial products. Find the product.

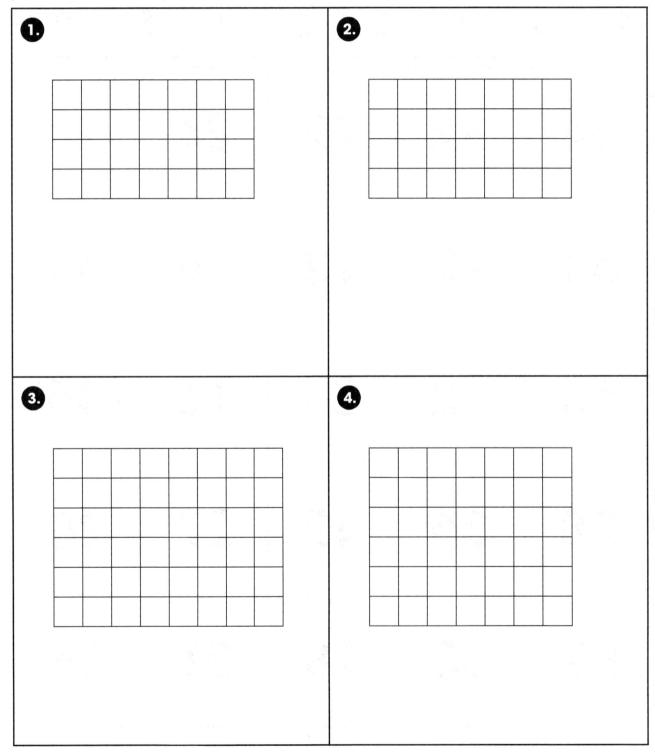

1.

2.

3.

4.

Math Games for the Common Core   © Didax — www.didax.com

"Using Facts You Know"
Recording Sheet – page 2 (Game 3-4)

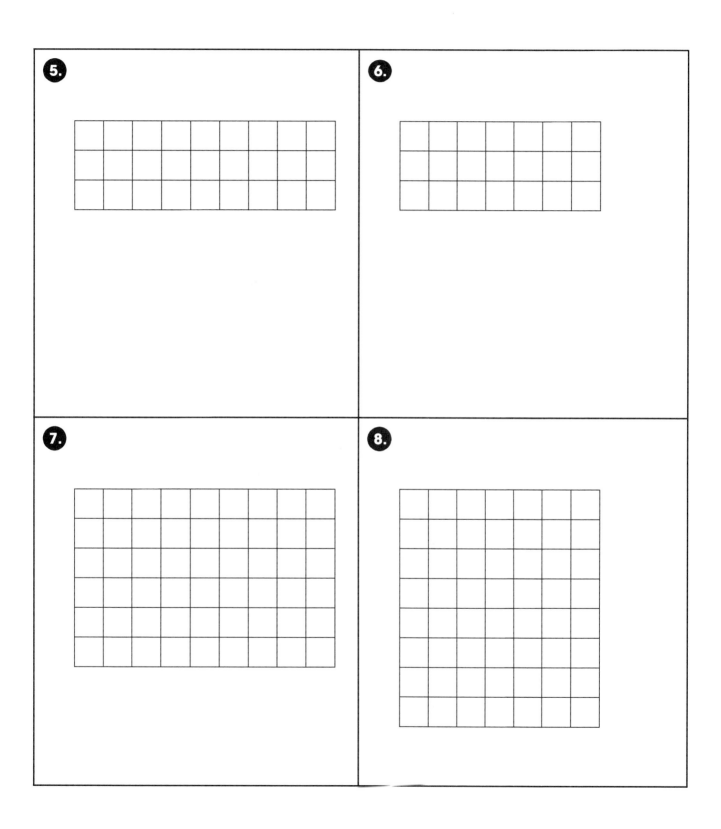

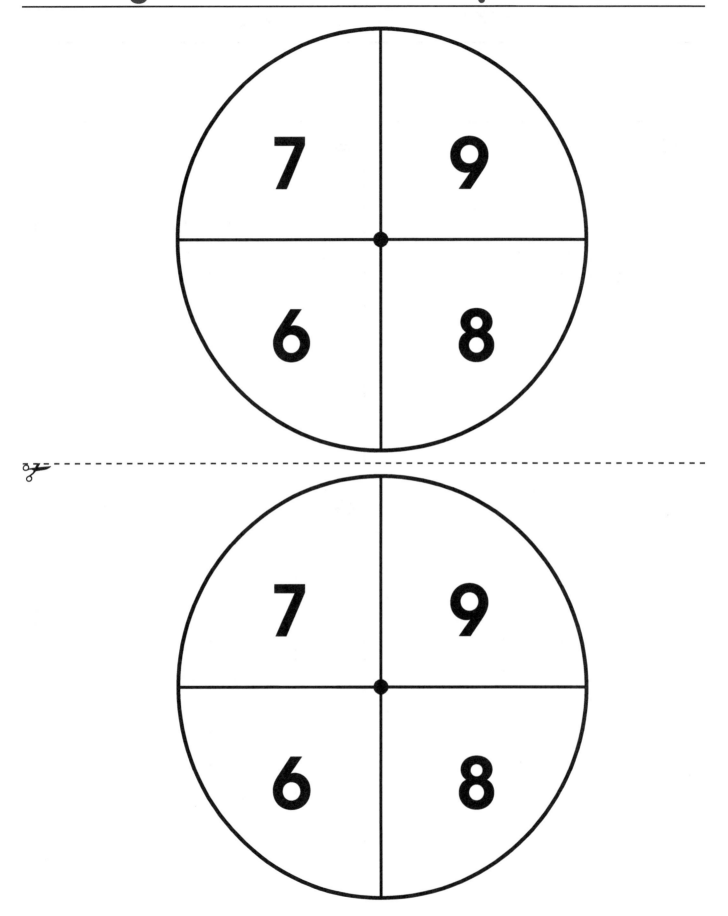

"Using Facts . . ." Game Board A (Game 3-4)

Use Number Cards:

Factors:

3	4	5	6	7	8	9

36	**24**	**32**	**64**	**49**
21	**45**	**49**	**24**	**56**
24	**42**	**28**	**48**	**27**
63	**36**	**56**	**30**	**42**
64	**72**	**28**	**36**	**48**

"Using Facts . . ." Game Board B (Game 3-4)

Use Number Cards:

Factors:

6	7	8

36	48	36	64	49
56	64	49	63	56
42	56	48	36	64
56	63	72	48	42
54	72	36	63	49

"Putting It All Together" Game Board A

(Game 3-5)

4	6	8	10	12	14	16	18	20
6	9	12	15	18	21	24	27	30
8	12	16	20	24	28	32	36	40
10	15	20	25	30	35	40	45	50
12	18	24	30	36	42	48	54	60
14	21	28	35	42	49	56	63	70
16	24	32	40	48	56	64	72	80
18	27	36	45	54	63	72	81	90
20	30	40	50	60	70	80	90	100

"Putting It All Together" Game Board B
(Game 3-5)

4	27	12	81	70	32	18	40	56
15	28	36	10	18	30	63	32	80
20	12	50	24	48	90	64	18	80
50	72	48	21	60	35	20	24	6
100	54	35	14	42	20	30	14	16
8	21	60	24	30	12	56	24	90
16	6	40	15	36	42	16	63	30
10	27	45	12	49	45	20	8	36
28	70	54	72	40	25	9	40	18

Spinner for the Divisor "2"

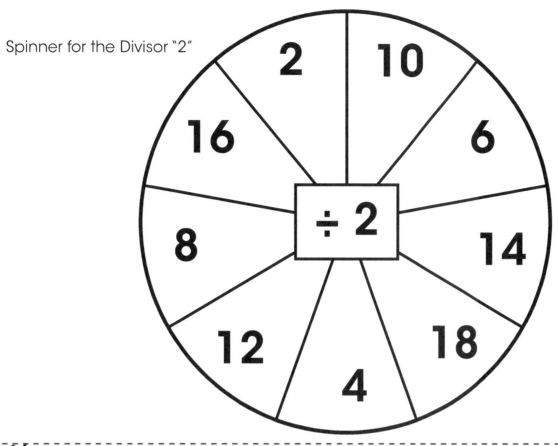

Spinner for the Divisor "3"

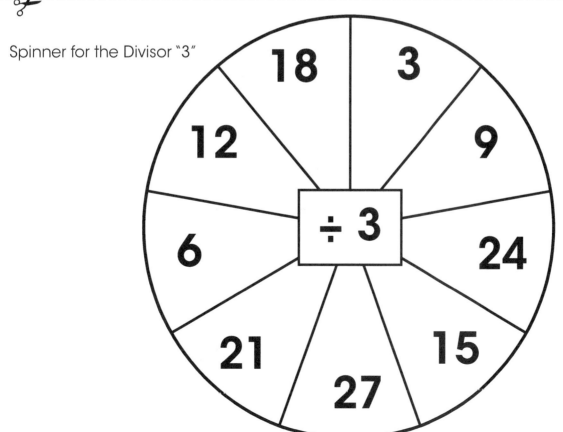

"Let's Divvy It Up" Spinners (Game 3-7)

Spinner for the Divisor "4"

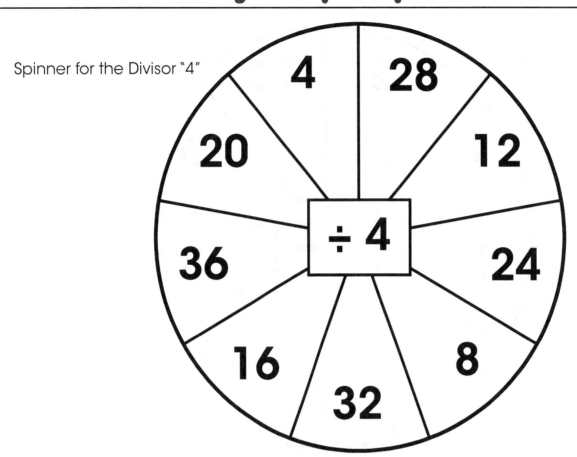

Spinner for the Divisor "5"

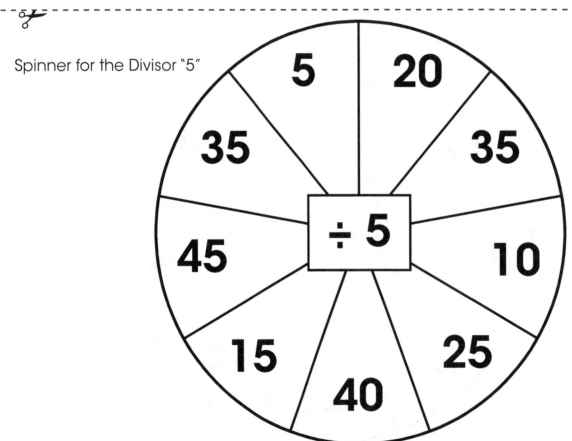

"Let's Divvy It Up" Spinners (Game 3-7)

Spinner for the Divisor "6"

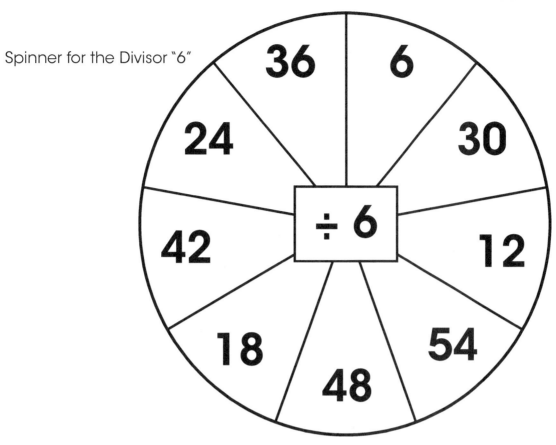

Spinner for the Divisor "7"

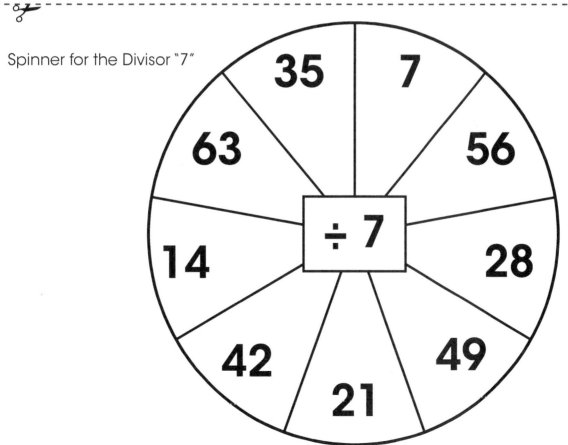

"Let's Divvy It Up" Spinners (Game 3-7)

Spinner for the Divisor "8"

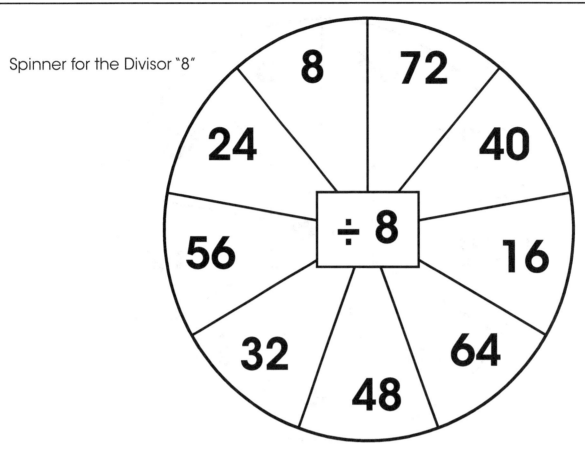

Spinner for the Divisor "9"

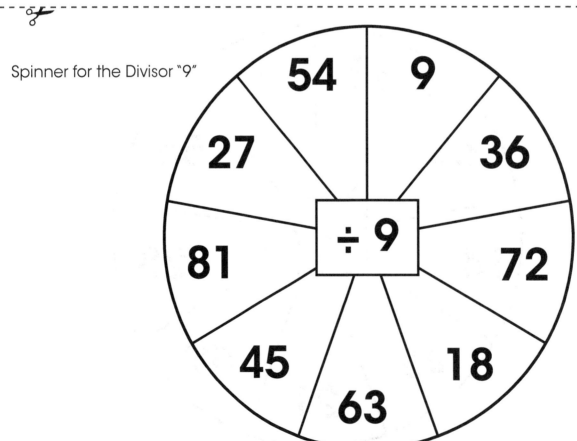

"Let's Divvy It Up" Spinners (Game 3-7)

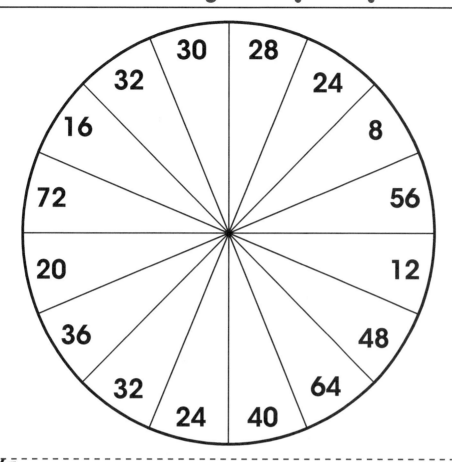

Spinner for Divisors "4" and "8"

Can you divide by 4 and get a 1-digit quotient?

or

Can you divide by 8 and get a 1-digit quotient?

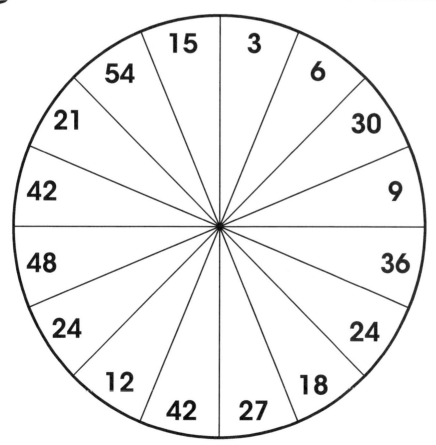

Spinner for Divisors "3" and "6"

Can you divide by 3 and get a 1-digit quotient?

or

Can you divide by 6 and get a 1-digit quotient?

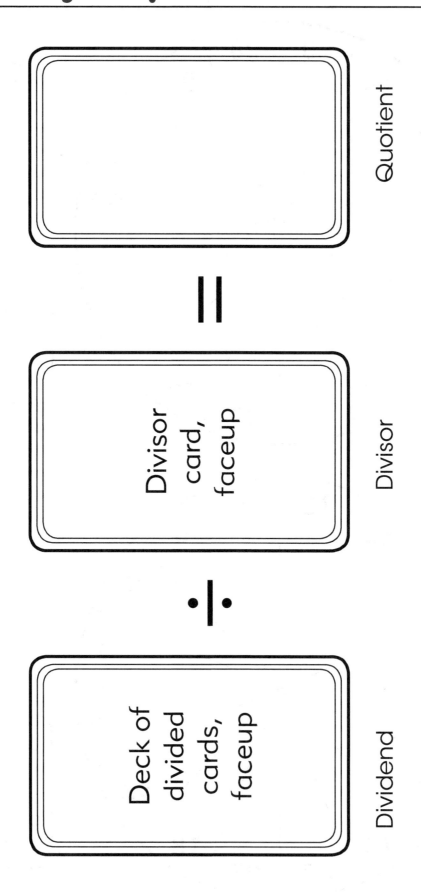

Quotient

=

Divisor card, faceup

Divisor

÷

Deck of divided cards, faceup

Dividend

"Let's Get A-Round to It" Table (Game 3-8)

List the three cards you drew: _____, _____, _____

All the Possible 3-Digit Numbers	Round to the Nearest 100	Round to the Nearest 10

List the three cards you drew: _____, _____, _____

All the Possible 3-Digit Numbers	Round to the Nearest 100	Round to the Nearest 10

List the three cards you drew: _____, _____, _____

All the Possible 3-Digit Numbers	Round to the Nearest 100	Round to the Nearest 10

"Let's Get A-Round to It" Game Board A
(Game 3-8)

10	20	30	40	50	60	70	80	90	100
110	120	130	140	150	160	170	180	190	200
210	220	230	240	250	260	270	280	290	300
310	320	330	340	350	360	370	380	390	400
410	420	430	440	450	460	470	480	490	500
510	520	530	540	550	560	570	580	590	600
610	620	630	640	650	660	670	680	690	700
710	720	730	740	750	760	770	780	790	800
810	820	830	840	850	860	870	880	890	900
910	920	930	940	950	960	970	980	990	1000

"Let's Get A-Round to It" Game Boards
B and C (Game 3-8)

Game Board B

10	20	30	40	50	60	70	80	90	100
10	20	30	40	50	60	70	80	90	100
10	20	30	40	50	60	70	80	90	100
10	20	30	40	50	60	70	80	90	100
10	20	30	40	50	60	70	80	90	100

Game Board C

100	200	300	400	500	600	700	800	900	1000
100	200	300	400	500	600	700	800	900	1000
100	200	300	400	500	600	700	800	900	1000
100	200	300	400	500	600	700	800	900	1000
100	200	300	400	500	600	700	800	900	1000

"The Multiples of 10" Game Board (Game 3-9)

40	60	80	100	120	140	160	180	200
60	90	120	150	180	210	240	270	300
80	120	160	200	240	280	320	360	400
100	150	200	250	300	350	400	450	500
120	180	240	300	360	420	480	540	600
140	210	280	350	420	490	560	630	700
160	240	320	400	480	560	640	720	800
180	270	360	450	540	630	720	810	900
200	300	400	500	600	700	800	900	1000

"That's 'Sum' Difference" Cards (Game 3-10)

Print 3 copies on card stock for each deck.

100	**100**	**100**	**100**
10	**10**	**10**	**10**
1	**1**	**1**	**1**

"That's 'Sum' Difference" Cards

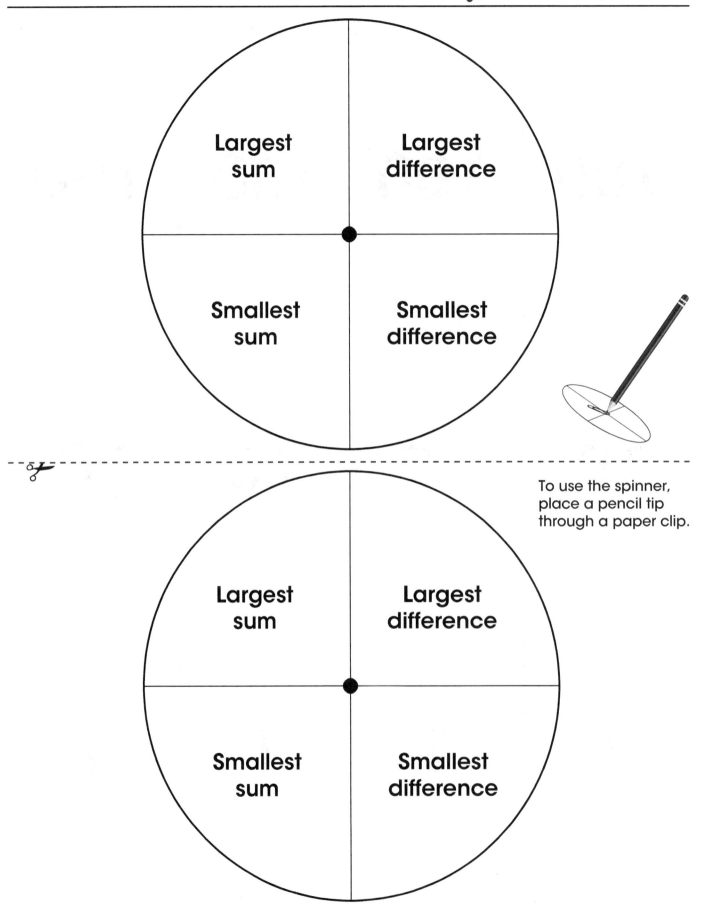

To use the spinner, place a pencil tip through a paper clip.

Write each fraction below the picture.

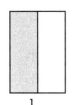

$$\frac{1}{2} = \frac{2}{4} = \underline{\quad\quad}$$

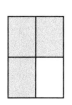 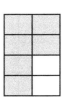

$$\frac{1}{4} = \underline{\quad\quad}$$

$$\underline{\quad\quad} = \underline{\quad\quad}$$

$$\underline{\quad\quad} = \underline{\quad\quad}$$

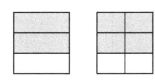

$$\underline{\quad\quad} = \underline{\quad\quad}$$

Write the fraction indicated by the arrow.

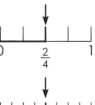

 _____

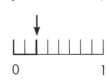 _____

 _____

 _____

 _____

 _____

 _____

 _____

"Match the Fractions" Notes – page 2 (Game 3-11)

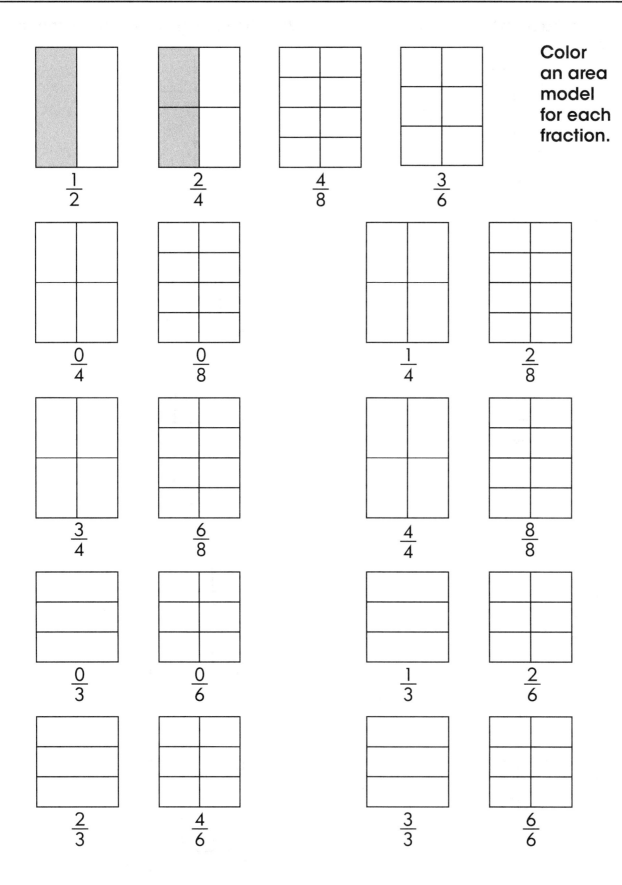

Color an area model for each fraction.

$\dfrac{1}{2}$ $\dfrac{2}{4}$ $\dfrac{4}{8}$ $\dfrac{3}{6}$

$\dfrac{0}{4}$ $\dfrac{0}{8}$ $\dfrac{1}{4}$ $\dfrac{2}{8}$

$\dfrac{3}{4}$ $\dfrac{6}{8}$ $\dfrac{4}{4}$ $\dfrac{8}{8}$

$\dfrac{0}{3}$ $\dfrac{0}{6}$ $\dfrac{1}{3}$ $\dfrac{2}{6}$

$\dfrac{2}{3}$ $\dfrac{4}{6}$ $\dfrac{3}{3}$ $\dfrac{6}{6}$

Math Games for the Common Core
© Didax — www.didax.com

Number Cards 0–10

0	1	2	3
4	5	6	7
8	9	10	

Used in Games 3-1 through 3-10.

Printing half of the decks on a different-color card stock will make cleanup easier.

Multiplication Chart

Used in Games 3-1 through 3-7.

×	0	1	2	3	4	5	6	7	8	9	10
0	0	0	0	0	0	0	0	0	0	0	0
1	0	1	2	3	4	5	6	7	8	9	10
2	0	2	4	6	8	10	12	14	16	18	20
3	0	3	6	9	12	15	18	21	24	27	30
4	0	4	8	12	16	20	24	28	32	36	40
5	0	5	10	15	20	25	30	35	40	45	50
6	0	6	12	18	24	30	36	42	48	54	60
7	0	7	14	21	28	35	42	49	56	63	70
8	0	8	16	24	32	40	48	56	64	72	80
9	0	9	18	27	36	45	54	63	72	81	90
10	0	10	20	30	40	50	60	70	80	90	100

Product/Dividend Cards – 1

Used in Games 3-6 and 3-7. Print one set on card stock for each pair of students.

12	14	16	18
21	24	27	28
32	36	42	48

Product/Dividend Cards – 2

Used in Games 3-6 and 3-7. Print one set on card stock for each pair of students.

49 | 54 | 56 | 63

64 | 72 | 81

Fraction Number Cards

Used in Games 3-11 and 3-12. Print 1 copy of this page on card stock for each deck.

$$\frac{0}{2} \qquad \frac{1}{2} \qquad \frac{2}{2} \qquad \frac{0}{4}$$

$$\frac{1}{4} \qquad \frac{2}{4} \qquad \frac{3}{4} \qquad \frac{4}{4}$$

$$\frac{0}{3} \qquad \frac{1}{3} \qquad \frac{2}{3} \qquad \frac{3}{3}$$

Fraction Number Cards

$$\frac{0}{6} \qquad \frac{1}{6} \qquad \frac{2}{6} \qquad \frac{3}{6}$$

$$\frac{4}{6} \qquad \frac{5}{6} \qquad \frac{6}{6} \qquad \frac{0}{8}$$

$$\frac{1}{8} \qquad \frac{2}{8} \qquad \frac{3}{8} \qquad \frac{4}{8}$$

Fraction Number Cards

$$\frac{5}{8} \qquad \frac{6}{8} \qquad \frac{7}{8} \qquad \frac{8}{8}$$

$$0 \qquad 1 \qquad \text{Wild Card} \qquad \text{Wild Card}$$

Wild Card | Wild Card | Wild Card | Wild Card

Fraction Picture Cards

Used in Games 3-11 and 3-12. Print 1 copy of this page on card stock for each deck.

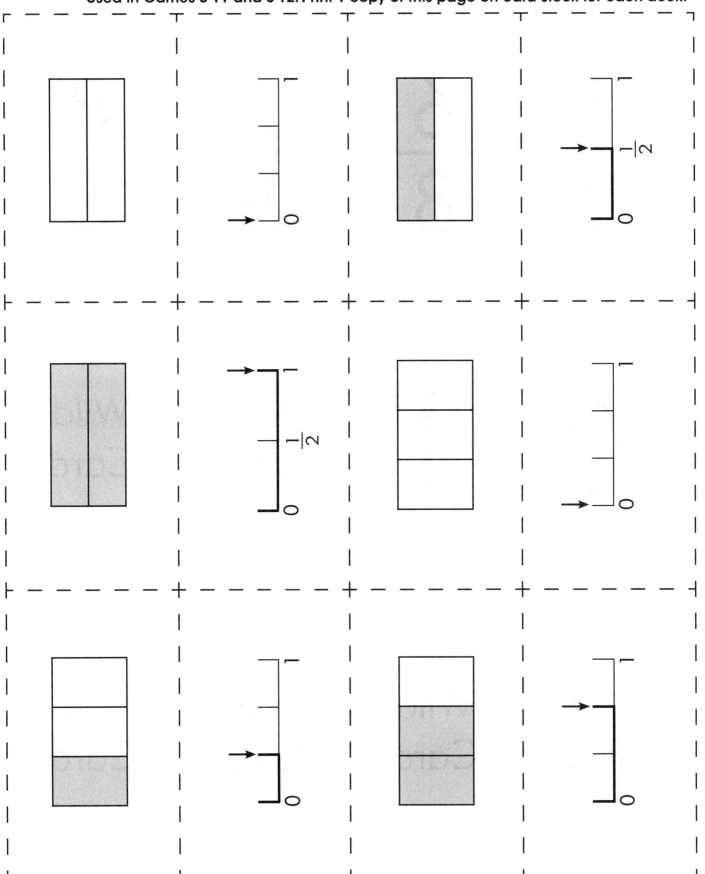

Fraction Picture Cards

Used in Games 3-11 and 3-12. Print 1 copy of this page on card stock for each deck.

Fraction Picture Cards

Used in Games 3-11 and 3-12. Print 1 copy of this page on card stock for each deck.

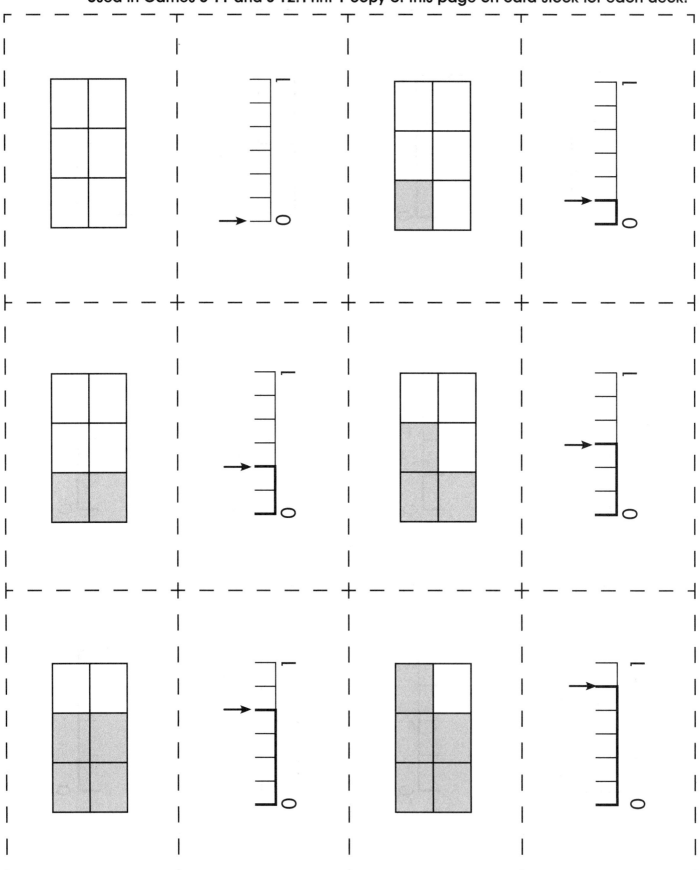

Math Games for the Common Core © Didax — www.didax.com

Fraction Picture Cards

Used in Games 3-11 and 3-12. Print 1 copy of this page on card stock for each deck.

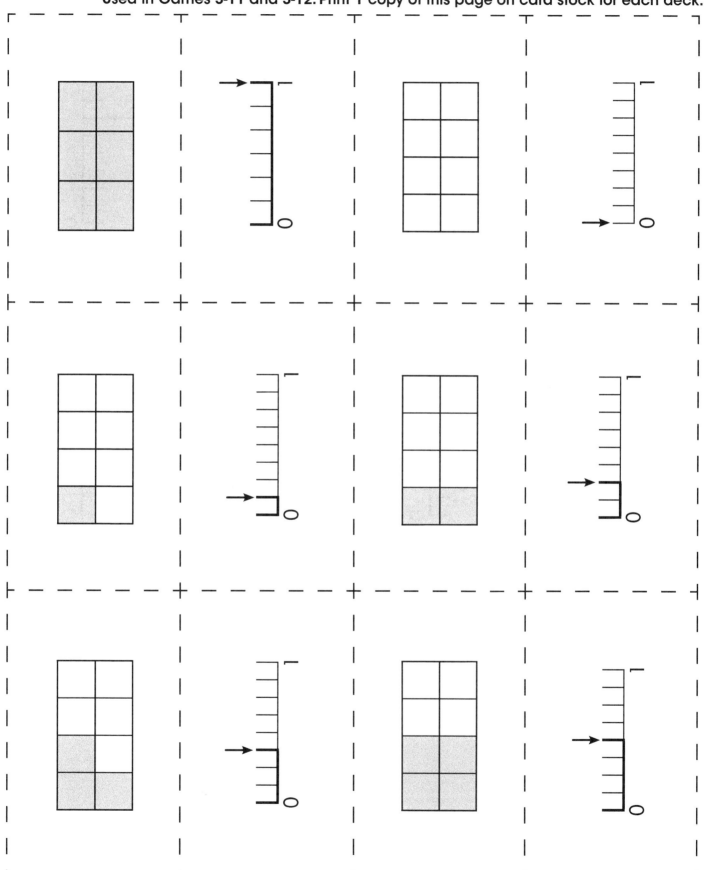

Fraction Picture Cards

Used in Games 3-11 and 3-12. Print 4 copies of this page on card stock for each deck.

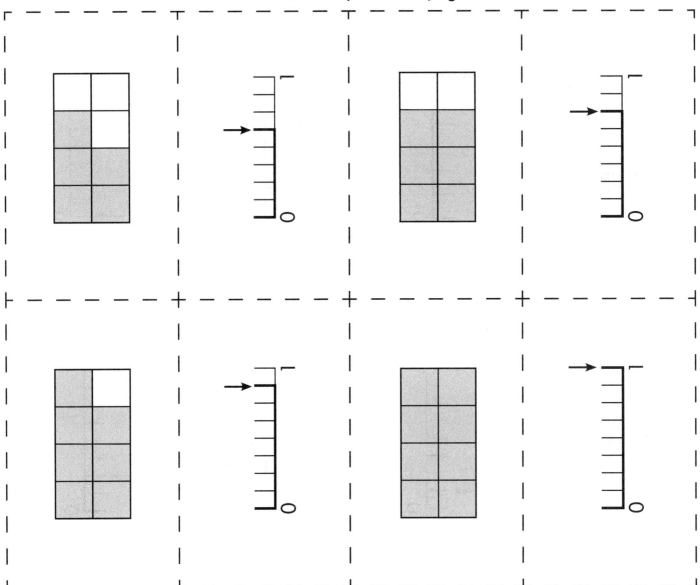

Game Rules

"Double Trouble" Game

Object: Multiply your "spinner number" by the number on your number card. The player with the larger (or smaller) product wins.

How to Play:

1. Players take turns. On your turn:

   • Spin the spinner to get your "spinner number."

   • Draw a number card from the deck.

   • Multiply the "spinner number" by the number on your card.

   • Say the equation. (For example, if you spin 2 and draw a 7, say: "2 times 7 equals 14.")

2. The player with the larger product wins both cards.

3. Repeat until the deck is used up. The player with the most cards wins.

4. Shuffle the cards and play again. This time the player with the smaller product wins both cards.

> ## Materials
> • "Double Trouble" Spinner
> • Deck of Number Cards 0–10
> • Multiplication Chart (facedown, except when used to check products)

Game Rules

"Double Trouble – Four in a Row" Game

Object: Use multiplication to capture four numbers in a row (horizontal, vertical, or diagonal) on the game board.

How to Play:

1. Players take turns drawing a number card.

2. On your turn:

   • Multiply the number on the card by one of the factors at the top of the page.

   • Say the multiplication fact and place a tile on the product on the game board.

3. If that product has already been captured, it is the other player's turn.

4. The first player to capture four numbers in a row wins. (The numbers have to be next to each other on the board.)

> **Materials**
> • "Double Trouble – Four in a Row" Game Board
> • 4 sets of the Number Cards 2 and 4
> • Tiles or other markers

Game Rules

"Think About 10" Game

Object: Multiply your "spinner number" by the number on your card. Larger (or smaller) product wins.

How to Play:

1. Players take turns. On your turn:

   • Spin the spinner to get your "spinner number."

   • Draw a number card from the deck.

   • Multiply the "spinner number" by the number on your card.

   • Say the equation. (For example, if you spin 9 and draw a 3, say: "9 times 3 equals 27.")

2. The player with the larger product wins both cards.

3. Repeat until the deck is used up. The player with the most cards wins.

4. Shuffle the cards and play again. This time the player with the smaller product wins both cards.

> **Materials**
> • "Think About 10" Spinner
> • Deck of Number Cards 0–10
> • Multiplication Chart (facedown, except when used to check products)

Game Rules

"Think About 10 – Four in a Row" Game

Object: Use multiplication to capture four numbers in a row (horizontal, vertical, or diagonal) on the game board.

How to Play:

1. Take turns drawing a card.

2. On your turn:

   • Multiply the number on the card by one of the factors at the top of the page.

   • Say the multiplication fact and find the product on the board. Place a tile on the product.

3. If that product has already been captured, it is the other player's turn.

4. The first player to capture four numbers in a row wins.

Materials
- 4 sets of the Number Cards 4, 5, 9, and 10
- "Think About 10 – Four in a Row" Game Board A
- "Think About 10 – Four in a Row" Game Board B (optional)
- Tiles or other markers

"Triple Trouble" Game

Object: Multiply your "spinner number" by the number on your card. Larger (or smaller) product wins.

Materials

- "Triple Trouble" Spinner
- Deck of Number Cards 0–10
- Multiplication Chart (facedown, except when used to check products)

How to Play:

1. Players take turns. On your turn:

   - Spin the spinner to get your "spinner number."

   - Draw a number card from the deck.

   - Multiply the "spinner number" by the number on your card.

   - Say the equation. (For example, if you spin 9 and draw a 7, say: "6 times 7 equals 42.")

2. The player with the larger product wins both cards.

3. Repeat until the deck is used up. The player with the most cards wins.

4. Shuffle the cards and play again. This time the player with the smaller product wins both cards.

Game Rules

"Triple Trouble – Four in a Row" Game

Object: Use multiplication to capture four numbers in a row (horizontal, vertical, or diagonal) on the game board.

How to Play:

1. Players take turns drawing a card.

2. On your turn:
   - Multiply the number on the card by one of the factors at the top of the page.
   - Say the multiplication fact and find the product on the board. Place a tile on the product.

3. If that product has already been captured, it is the other player's turn.

4. The first player to capture four numbers in a row wins.

Materials
- "Triple Trouble – Four in a Row" Game Board A
- Deck of Number Cards 2–9
- Tiles or other markers
- Game Boards B and C (optional)

GAME 3–4

"Using Facts You Know" Game

Object: Multiply your "spinner number" by the number on your card. Larger (or smaller) product wins.

How to Play:

1. Players take turns. On your turn:

   • Spin the spinner to get your "spinner number."

   • Draw a number card from the deck.

   • Multiply the "spinner number" by the number on your card.

   • Say the equation. (For example, if you spin 7 and draw a 4, say: "7 times 4 equals 28.")

2. The player with the larger product wins both cards.

3. Repeat until the deck is used up. The player with the most cards wins.

4. Shuffle the cards and play again. This time the player with the smaller product wins both cards.

Materials

• "Using Facts You Know" Spinner

• Deck of Number Cards 0–10

• Multiplication Chart (facedown, except when used to check products)

Game Rules

"Using Facts You Know – Four in a Row" Game

Object: Use multiplication to capture four numbers in a row (horizontal, vertical, or diagonal) on the game board.

Materials
- "Using Facts You Know – Four in a Row" Game Board A
- 4 sets of Number Cards 6, 7, 8, and 9
- Tiles or other markers
- Game Board B (optional)

How to Play:

1. Players take turns drawing a card.

2. On your turn:

   - Multiply the number on the card by one of the factors at the top of the page.

   - Say the multiplication fact and find the product on the board. Place a tile on the product.

3. If that product has already been captured, it is the other player's turn.

4. The first player to capture four numbers in a row wins.

Game Rules

"Putting It All Together" Game

Object: Multiply two numbers to "capture" a number on the game board. The first player to capture three sets of three numbers in a row (horizontal, vertical, or diagonal) wins.

Materials

- "Putting It All Together" Game Board A
- Deck of Number Cards 2–10
- Colored pencils or markers
- Game Board B (optional)

How to Play:

1. Decide which of you will be the dealer. The dealer deals five cards to both of you.

2. On your turn:

   - Multiply two of your cards together to "capture" a number on the game board.

   - Mark that square with "your" color, and discard those two cards.

   - Draw two new cards.

3. Instead of capturing a number, you may discard all five cards and draw new cards. Then your turn is over.

4. The first player to capture three sets of three numbers in a row wins the game.

Game Rules

"Is That a Fact?" Game

Object: Figure out the unseen number on your forehead while seeing your partner's number and the product of the two numbers.

Materials
- Deck of Number Cards 0–9
- Multiplication Chart for the captain to use, if needed (otherwise, keep facedown)
- Paper and pencil

How to Play:

1. Decide which of you will be the captain.

2. The captain says, "Salute," and the other two players each put a card on their own forehead. (Make sure not to look at the card before you put it on your forehead.)

3. If you are the captain, say and write the product of the two numbers.

4. If you are a crewmember, keep your card on your forehead until you have figured out what number is on your card.

5. The first crewmember to correctly say his/her own number wins one point.

6. Play more rounds. The crewmember who has the most points at the end of the game wins.

Game Rules

"Let's Divvy It Up" Game

Object: Collect the most dividend cards by correctly dividing.

How to Play:

1. Place the divisor and dividend card decks on the game board. Place one divisor card faceup.

2. Take turns. On your turn, divide the dividend by the divisor, if possible.

3. If the cards on the board can be used to make a division fact (for example, 42 and 6), say the division fact: "42 divided by 6 equals 7."

4. If your division fact is correct, put the dividend card in your "win pile." Then it is the other player's turn.

5. If the cards on the board cannot be used to make a division fact, draw a new divisor card and divide it into the number on the dividend card. If the new card cannot be used, your turn is over.

6. Play continues until all the dividend cards are used. The player with the most cards wins the game.

Materials

- Deck of Number Cards 2–9 (remove the 5), called "divisor cards"
- Deck of Product/Dividend Cards, called "dividend cards"
- "Let's Divvy It Up" Game Board

Game Rules

"Let's Get A-Round to It" Game

Object: Round three-digit numbers to the nearest 10 or nearest 100 to capture three sets of three numbers in a row (horizontal, vertical, or diagonal).

How to Play:

1. Players take turns. On your turn:

   • Draw four cards.

   • Select three of those cards to create a three-digit number. (Zero may be the first digit.)

   • Round the number to the nearest 10 or nearest 100. Use your colored pencil to mark (capture) the number on the game board.

   • Discard all four cards.

2. The first player to capture three sets of three numbers in a row wins.

Materials
- "Let's Get A-Round to It" Game Board A
- Deck of Number Cards 0–9
- Colored pencils or markers
- Game Boards B and C (optional)

10	20	30	40	50	60	70	80	90	100
110	120	130	140	150	160	170	180	190	200
210	220	230	240	250	260	270	280	290	300
310	320	330	340	350	360	370	380	390	400
410	420	430	440	450	460	470	480	490	500
510	520	530	540	550	560	570	580	590	600
610	620	630	640	650	660		680	690	700
710	720	730	740	750	760	77	780	790	800
810	820	830	840	850	860	870		890	900
910	920	930	940	950	960	970	980		1000

Game Rules

"The Multiples of 10" Game

Object: Multiply a one-digit number by a multiple of 10 to capture three sets of three numbers in a row (horizontal, vertical, or diagonal).

Materials
- "The Multiples of 10" Game Board
- Deck of Number Cards 2–9
- "× 10" index card
- Colored markers

How to Play:

1. Decide who is going to be the dealer. The dealer deals five cards to each player.

2. On your turn:

   - Choose two cards and use the "× 10" card to create a multiplication expression. Say the expression and solve it.

     Example: You choose the cards 5 and 3. Place the "× 10" card next to the 5 to make 50. Then say the expression "50 × 3" and solve it ("50 × 3" = 150).

   - Mark ("capture") the product on the board.

   - Discard the two number cards and draw two new cards.

3. The first player to capture three sets of three numbers in a row wins.

Game Rules

That's "Sum" Difference (Game 3-10)

Object: Create the sum or difference that best matches the target. The player with the answer closest to the target wins a chip. The player with the most chips wins the game.

Materials
- Deck of Number Cards 0–9 (page 107)
- Spinner (page 104)
- Chips or counters
- Student-made double place value mats (Fold 11 × 17-in. paper into thirds and cut in half—"hotdog fold"—for two mats.)

How to Play:

1. One of you spins the spinner to decide the "target" for the game (for example: "Largest sum").

2. Draw and place one card at a time on the place value mat to make a three-digit number. Once you place a card, it can't be moved. Do not use zero in the hundreds place.

3. Draw a fourth card. You can use it to replace one of the cards on your mat or discard it.

4. Repeat steps 1 and 2 to make a second three-digit number.

5. Add or subtract the two numbers you have created according to the spinner target. Record your work.

   (*Note:* When subtracting, make sure to subtract the smaller number from the larger number.)

6. The player with the sum or difference closest to the target wins a chip.

Match The Fractions (Game 3-11)

Object: Collect pairs of equivalent fractions.

How to Play:

1. Decide who is going to be the dealer. The dealer deals three cards to each player.

2. On your turn:

   • Draw one or more cards from the deck until you can make an equivalent pair.

   • Say the equation (for example, "$\frac{1}{2} = \frac{2}{4}$") and put those cards in your win pile.

3. Keep playing until you or your partner goes out or until the deck is used up.

4. Subtract the number of cards still in your hand from your win pile to get your final score.

Materials

• Deck of Fraction Number Cards and whole numbers 0 and 1 (Remove 1/6, 5/6, 1/8, 3/8, 5/8, 7/8.)

• Completed Fraction Notes pages (optional) – for reference

Game Rules

Wild Card Fractions (Game 3-12)

Object: Win the most cards by comparing fractions and explaining comparisons.

How to Play:

1. Each player draws five cards. Place a privacy barrier between you. Take turns going first.

2. Player 1: Put a card on the table. (Do not lead with a wild card.)

3. Player 2: Put a card on the table that matches either the numerator or the denominator of Player 1's card. You may use a wild card to represent a specific fraction.

4. Player 2: If you have no card to play, draw cards until you can play.

5. Players flip a coin (heads: larger fraction wins; tails: smaller fraction wins).

6. The winner explains why his/her fraction is larger (or smaller) than the other player's. If correct, the winner puts both cards in his/her "win pile."

7. If the two fractions are equivalent (the same size), play again. The winner takes all four cards from that round.

8. Keep playing until all cards have been played or until a player is stuck. The player with the most "win pile" cards wins the game.

> **Materials**
> - Deck of Fraction Number Cards and 6 wild cards
> - Coin
> - Two privacy barriers
> - Completed Fraction Notes pages from Game 3-11 (optional)

Math Games for the Common Core